A Room to Learn:

Rethinking Classroom Environments

Pamela Evanshen
Janet Faulk

Acknowledgments

During the past 10 years, many teachers, administrators, and children have contributed to this text. We have enjoyed collaborating and reflecting with these partners in the education of young children. We appreciate their willingness to open their classrooms and schools to our visits. Without the support of our teacher friends, we would not have been able to capture the practices and processes associated with using the environment as a teaching tool. We can't thank you enough for your time, dedication, and photographs.

We extend a special thanks to the teachers who welcomed and collaborated with us during the classroom make-over process. We are grateful for the technical assistance from our graduate assistants and for the early childhood education students who contributed many long hours on the classroom environment projects.

Many thanks to the administrators who are truly leaders in creating positive learning environments for all children. We admire your strength to do what is right for children and your support of teachers in primary classrooms.

Thanks to our professional colleagues in higher education for their support throughout this project. In addition, we thank Dr. Rebecca Isbell for inspiring us through her work on preschool learning environments.

Finally, we send our gratitude and love to our families. Thanks for your support, understanding, and patience during this journey.

Thank you to all who have participated in this journey!

Janet Faulk   *Pamela Evanshen*

A Room To LEARN

Rethinking Classroom Environments

Featuring Before and After Photos!

Pamela Evanshen
and Janet Faulk

Bulk purchase
Gryphon House books are available for special premiums and sales promotions as well as for fund-raising use. Special editions or book excerpts also can be created to specification. For details, contact the Director of Marketing at Gryphon House.

Disclaimer
Gryphon House, Inc. and the authors cannot be held responsible for damage, mishap, or injury incurred during the use of or because of activities in this book. Appropriate and reasonable caution and adult supervision of children involved in activities and corresponding to the age and capability of each child involved is recommended at all times. Do not leave children unattended at any time. Observe safety and caution at all times.

A Room to Learn: Rethinking Classroom Environments
Pamela Evanshen and Janet Faulk
© 2011 Pamela Evanshen and Janet Faulk

Published by Gryphon House, Inc.
10770 Columbia Pike, Suite 201
Silver Spring, MD 20901
800.638.0928; 301.595.9500; 301.595.0051 (fax)

Visit us on the web at www.gryphonhouse.com

Library of Congress Cataloging-in-Publication Information
Evanshen, Pamela.
A room to learn : rethinking classroom environments / Pamela Evanshen, Janet Faulk.
  p. cm.
ISBN 978-0-87659-315-8
1. Language arts (Elementary) 2. Classroom environment. 3. Reflective teaching. 4. Educational evaluation. I. Title.
LB1576.E89 2011
371.102'4--dc22
                          2011011475

Table of Contents

Preface

Our ideas about the way children grow and learn are informed by our study of current research, by our interactions with teachers and administrators in school settings, by our own experiences as teachers and administrators, and by our observations of young learners. As a result, we have developed an educational philosophy shaped by the teaching and learning principles associated with constructivism, and a practice influenced by our experiences with real teachers, real administrators, and real children.

We believe that the learning environment is the foundational element for the teaching and learning processes that take place in the classroom. We concur with Eric Jensen (2003) who said, *"At school only the quality of the teacher is a greater determinant of student success than the environment. One environment brings out the best in us and another brings out the worst in us. They can be nourishing or toxic, supportive or draining. Environments are never neutral. How important are they? How important is water to fish?"* (p. v).

Pam's Reflections

The purpose of writing this book is to share my passion for what education can look like and feel like for elementary-aged children, especially those in public schools. With my training in early childhood, special education, and elementary education, I have had the opportunity to experience three different teacher-preparation and administrative-preparation programs. In each program, there was a distinct lack of emphasis on how to use the classroom environment as a teaching tool. In my professional experience as a teacher and administrator in these various education programs, as well as in my work as an education consultant and college professor, it has become increasingly clear to me that educators often use lecture, whole group, and worksheet-driven formats, even though such formats may not be in the best interest of the children or the educators. Interestingly, my research and experience also make it clear that many educators do not necessarily want to teach this way. Rather, these educators didn't receive comprehensive training to explore more innovative educational practices. Even in school systems that do try to provide teachers with up-to-date training based on the latest research and innovations, there appears to be a disconnect between the new methodologies and the classroom environments that most teachers set up and use to teach.

I believe the classroom environment is the foundation for quality teaching and learning. I also believe that **all** children can learn. I do not, however, believe that all children can learn the same thing, at the same time, during the same week, on the same page, in the same manner. I believe we need to let go of the notion that the curriculum is born of the textbook and the textbook is the sole tool for teaching and learning. I believe a child's environment should be the textbook. I believe the environment facilitates learning. I believe that learning happens and becomes meaningful if the environment is designed appropriately to facilitate learning! I also believe it can motivate educators to grow professionally when they use the environment as a teaching tool. A successful professional educator consistently examines the teaching strategies she uses, and continuously explores learning opportunities in an effort to expand her own knowledge base. The successful educator does this in order to provide quality learning experiences for *all* children. Utilizing the environment as a teaching tool can help every teacher meet the needs of *all* the children in her class.

My mission is to change the face of elementary education: what it looks like, feels like, and what the experience is like for elementary-aged children and their teachers, especially those in K–3 classrooms. I hope that this book will serve as a tool for K–3 teachers, administrators, teacher educators, and those providing professional development for early educators. My hope is that primary teachers will use this book to self-assess and reflect upon their classroom environments and how those environments function as teaching tools that can have a profound impact upon the success with which children develop the skills necessary to become responsible individual and collaborative learners.

Janet's Reflections

It is my great joy to be an educator. I have had the opportunity to work with colleagues who are dedicated to the profession and to the children who are in their care. It has been my privilege to have known many excellent teachers whose classrooms were vibrant, caring communities of learning. Through these experiences, I have seen the impact that nurturing, well-designed environments have in the quality of a child's education. As educators, we have a moral imperative to provide all our children with the best education possible. *All* children deserve a high quality education in an emotionally and physically safe environment. *All* children deserve teachers who understand developmentally appropriate practice and who design classrooms that reflect a commitment to creating a child-centered learning community. *All* children deserve an education that focuses on helping them develop into life-long learners and contributors to society.

In my capacity as an administrator and as a college professor, I have had the opportunity to work with dozens of teachers to design effective, meaningful instruction for our children. I believe that one of the great disappointments of our profession is the gap that exists between knowing and doing in many of our early childhood classrooms. While the research that highlights the importance and value of best practices continues to grow, both qualitatively and quantitatively, too often, the pedagogy we see in our classrooms does not reflect this body of research.

This book aims to bridge that gap between knowing and doing. It creates a map for educators to follow when designing a classroom that will engage young learners. This book collects the results of 10 years of research spent asking two vital educational questions: "What do I do to ensure that my legacy will be children who become life-long learners?" and, "What do I do to provide the educational environment—social, emotional, physical, and intellectual—that will maximize the time my children are engaged in meaningful work?"

Purpose of the Book

This book can serve as a tool to guide an individual teacher, small group of teachers, whole school, or school system to higher levels of performance. It provides not only theory, research, and principles of best practices in primary classrooms, but also offers concrete suggestions for using the environment as a teaching tool. The information in this book can benefit both beginning and experienced teachers as they design their classroom environments. The thoughtful professor can use this book as a resource for informing teacher practice because it includes the philosophical and instructional principles which guide the early childhood educator.

The ultimate goal of teaching is to engage the learner in meaningful work that leads to understanding. Often, this results in a shift in the teacher's role from one that is teacher-centered to one that is more child-centered. We hope this book will help educators to do two important things in their classrooms: 1) use the learning environment as a teaching tool, and 2) utilize a variety of teaching strategies within the newly designed environment to ensure children and educators remain engaged throughout the learning process.

Introduction

The classroom environments we create often reflect our beliefs about teaching and learning. It is important to take the time to consider both our classroom design and our practice, asking ourselves, "What do I believe about teaching and learning?" The answer to this question can help us analyze our classroom environment in thoughtful and reflective ways. Too often, we find a disconnect between teachers' belief systems and the structures for learning they incorporate into their classrooms. The classroom environment is a powerful tool for the teacher. It can either support or impede a teacher's goal for active child participation. Chapters 1 and 2 of this book highlights research that explores the benefits of designing classrooms to emphasize child-centered learning. It includes the *philosophical foundation*, (associated with the theories of Piaget, Vygotsky, and Dewey) coupled with the *instructional foundation*, (teaching/learning cycles and best practices for teaching and learning).

Chapters 3–8 offers educators ways to facilitate the reflection, planning, and action necessary to utilize the educational environment as a teaching tool. The *Primary Educator's Environment Checklist* (see page 181) helps identify areas of focus for classroom development. Chapters 3–8 each describe a specific component of the checklist, such as nourishment, use of color and plants, room arrangement, learning centers, and the impact of clutter on the learning environment. Of great help are "before" and "after" photographs of real classrooms. These illustrate the various ways educators, after learning about the importance of the classroom environment, changed their classroom design in order to use the environment as a teaching tool. Chapter 9 highlights inquiry-based learning with examples from classrooms where teachers effectively use their environment as a teaching tool. Each chapter concludes with comments from teachers, consultants, and principals about the ideas covered in that chapter. These comments come from conversations, workshops, and professional development sessions we have run regarding the importance of classroom environments.

Over the course of this book, we hope you see what an effective teaching tool the classroom environment can be, and begin exploring ways to construct your classroom to facilitate engaged learning for all the children in your class.

Using the Environment as a Teaching Tool:

The Philosophical Foundation

The Philosophical Foundation

The way teachers organize early childhood classrooms reflects their understanding of the ways children learn as well as the structures teachers believe will support children in that learning. To reflect on the quality of classroom environments, it is helpful to look at the work of theorists and school reform practitioners—particularly Jean Piaget (1896–1980), Lev Vygotsky (1896–1934), and John Dewey (1859–1952)—who have written about this very subject. Their work focuses on three specific issues that are of concern here:

- The characteristics of the learner,
- The curricular content, and
- The instructional strategies which are used as a structure for learning.

Classrooms based on the work of Piaget, Dewey, and Vygotsky operate under the philosophy of teaching and learning called *constructivism*. Teachers support children's development by thoughtfully tailoring the environment and activities to promote the children's engagement in active learning (Bredekamp & Copple, 1997).

Below are introductions to the thinking of these three theorists, followed by an explanation of how the ideas apply to the classroom in the 21st century.

Jean Piaget

Piaget's theory of cognitive development describes how children create knowledge. Piaget's first three stages of cognitive development are: sensorimotor, preoperational, and concrete operations. According to Piaget, these stages describe how knowledge develops in young children, from birth through age eight. In addition, Piaget emphasizes the importance the educational environment plays in children's construction of knowledge (Piaget, 1963).

During these first three stages of cognitive development, Piaget suggests that children experience learning through their senses, manipulation of objects, direct experiences, and real experiences. Piaget's theory encourages the organization of classrooms that promote exploration, inquiry, and problem-solving. In inquiry-based classrooms teachers ask questions to extend the thinking, offer opportunities for social learning, encourage the exploration of ideas, and celebrate learning through documenting the process and then sharing that documentation with one another and those who visit the classroom.

Historically, the pedagogical approach has been to "instruct" our learners. This means that educators create a classroom design that consists of a large amount of space for teacher work, plus large group instructional areas, desks in rows, and little or no space for "construction" of knowledge, or active "playing with and sharing of knowledge." This design lends itself to worksheet-driven curricula and factual recall rather than total engagement.

If our goal in education is for children to engage in learning, develop higher-order thinking skills, think, reflect, and understand, then those children need opportunities to "play" with learning in a classroom environment. This environment needs to support each individual child and encourage engagement in meaningful work that can lead to higher-level thinking.

"Adaptation involves the processes of assimilation and accommodation. It is the way in which an individual adjusts to his environment. First he gathers ideas, information, perceptions, and experiences into existing mental models. This first step is assimilation. Accommodation is the modification of new information and actions to form a new mental plan or schema" (Singer & Revenson, 1996, p. 127). If, according to this definition, children adapt when they achieve a sense of equilibrium (or when they achieve a balance between assimilation and accommodation) then it is in the state of disequilibrium that educators can motivate learning. When children in the classroom are in a state of disequilibrium, educators can guide their development, appreciate their sense of wonder, and celebrate their curiosity by focusing on the following elements identified by Piaget: emotions, maturation, experience, and social interaction (Singer & Revenson, 1996). The physical classroom environment must have dynamic, non-traditional design in order to allow children to question, explore, search for answers, and express themselves during this state of disequilibrium. Educators must provide active and social learning experiences that support and encourage children's learning. These, in turn, lead to adaptation and understanding.

Lev Vygotsky

Lev Vygotsky's social development theory emphasizes that social interaction plays a fundamental role in the development of cognition (1962). He theorized that people learn first through person-to-person interactions and then individually through internalization processes that lead to deeper understanding (Vygotsky, 1978). When teachers plan the physical design of the classroom and the lessons to follow, does the physical design of the room allow for social interaction, a key component for cognitive development? Traditionally designed classrooms, where children work individually to complete assigned tasks, do not support Vygotsky's (1978) idea that the range of skills children can develop with adult guidance or peer collaboration exceeds the range of skills children can develop when learning alone.

Vygotsky believed that social interaction helps children construct knowledge. An effective learning environment should allow for child-to-child and adult-to-child interactions. Teachers need to be able to observe children so that they can identify what Vygotsky calls the Zone of Proximal Development (ZPD). Vygotsky describes the ZPD as the distance between the developmental level reached by independent problem-solving and the potential developmental level that can be reached through problem-solving under adult guidance or in collaboration with more capable peers (Vygotsky, 1978, p.86). The scaffolding, or support, that adults and peers provide can advance children's knowledge. Adult-to-child and child-to-child interactions are necessary for a classroom environment to generate this type of support.

John Dewey

John Dewey's approach to educational processes, developed in the early 1900s, is evident throughout early childhood education literature and is found in many contemporary classroom settings. Inherent to Dewey's philosophy of education is the belief that knowledge results from experience. His philosophy of teaching and learning focuses on the continuous interaction between past experiences and current situations. Learning does not occur in isolation. According to Dewey (1938/1997), the education process is continuous, so that each experience impacts the experiences that follow. Children respond to learning opportunities based not only upon the structure and presentation of a lesson, but also in relation to the children's previous experiences with related lessons.

Dewey (1916) recognized that each person has unique experiences and individual responses to those experiences. He also acknowledged that some experiences are detrimental to the developmental process while others are supportive. Dewey (1899) was convinced that the role of the teacher was not to stand and deliver instruction but to facilitate the learning process. His belief was that it should be the goal of the teacher to foster positive development of children in order to help them achieve their potential.

Quality educational design, in Dewey's terms, is learner-centered and offers experiences that address children's personal areas of interest. The effective teacher knows her learners and can structure connected and authentic learning experiences that will support their development. Dewey (1916) supports the use of classroom designs that foster experiential learning. One type of experiential learning frequently implemented in K–3 education, for example, is project-based learning (PBL). PBL reflects Dewey's philosophy that learning is not a static experience where children are recipients of knowledge; rather, project-based learning links knowledge with action. Through many connected experiences, the teacher guides the child to become an independent learner.

Dewey (1916) valued the social dynamic of education and its role in supporting the democratic society. He recognized that experiential learning could be a unifying agent for society because children develop interdependence through their common experiences.

The teacher is responsible for structuring the classroom environment in such a way that it helps children develop a sense of personal ownership of and responsibility to a democratic society, as well as develop an understanding of how they contribute to that society. A classroom that reflects Dewey's principles is one in which children not only interact with the learning activities but also with one another, creating common understandings and shared experiences.

21st Century

The knowledge and skills necessary for success in the 21st century are different from those needed in previous centuries. Therefore, classroom environments and pedagogy (how teachers teach) must change. This shift from what teachers have considered traditional to non-traditional or more constructivist educational approaches should guide teachers' efforts to prepare children for success in the global world. By incorporating early childhood principles in the primary grades and designing quality learning environments to include the social, emotional, and academic realms of teaching and learning, school leaders and teachers can develop citizens of the 21st century (Evanshen, 2010). The 21st Century Model for Teaching and Learning and Educational Change involves the Three *Es*: Environment, Engagement, and Enhancement.

Begin with the first *E*, transforming the foundation, the Environment. Move from a traditional physical design, with desks arranged in rows for large group instruction, to a non-traditional or more constructivist physical design, with more varied seating choices and work areas, as well as individual, small group, and large group meeting spaces. This non-traditional environment allows educators to move from a traditional pedagogy—in which the primary method of instruction is a teacher transfering or presenting knowledge to a large group of children—to a non-traditional or more constructivist, interactive pedagogy, where teachers and children work together to construct knowledge. The environment contributes to socialization, movement, and playing with learning so children can construct knowledge, understand concepts, and develop skills.

The second *E* involves transforming the classroom culture: Engagement. Once the foundation is in place, teachers can work on building a community in the classroom. This involves establishing routines and procedures, working together, reflecting, and sharing. Creating a positive climate and culture in the classroom, one in which children feel safe to take risks and share their thoughts and ideas, leads children to become engaged learners.

The third *E* involves transforming the academic approach: Enhancement. Enhancement occurs when content is meaningful to the individual learner as well as to the group. The elements necessary to transform the academic approach include: integrating instruction; utilizing assessment to guide planning and instruction; incorporating real experiences to allow for individual learning styles, intelligences, and preferences; and documenting the learning to guide and engage in reflective practice (Evanshen, 2010). One of the goals of this book is to serve as a tool for educators to use on the journey of designing classrooms and developing pedagogy for primary school learners of the 21st century.

Table I | 21st Century Model for Teaching and Learning and Educational Change

Transform the Foundation
ENVIRONMENT

Transform the Classroom Culture
ENGAGEMENT

Transform the Academic Approach
ENHANCEMENT

(Evanshen, 2010)

Using the Environment as a Teaching Tool:
The Instructional Foundation

CHAPTER 2

Teaching and Learning Cycles

Teachers must have an in-depth understanding of the ways in which children learn. This understanding provides a foundation for effective instruction and leads teachers to design their classrooms with multiple levels of educational support. One tool that can be useful in managing the learning process is the teaching-learning cycle. Using the teaching-learning cycle to guide instruction helps teachers make connections between the various aspects of the learning environment and children's mastery of curricular concepts. The teaching-learning cycle has been described by numerous researchers and practitioners, many of whom have designed models for depicting the stages of learning, the processes associated with learning, or the order of presentation of content knowledge.

Using a Framework

The consistent use of a framework for instruction supports children's educational development in settings from Pre-K to grade 3. The importance of using the teaching-learning cycle has been highlighted by Newmann, Smith, Allensworth, and Bryk (2001), whose research finds that programs offering connections across grade levels support child motivation. Children demonstrate greater feelings of self-efficacy when they understand how experiences and learning from one year relate to those of successive years. Schools with instructional coherence and articulation of strategies across the grade levels provide a meaningful context for teaching and learning.

Complete Act of Thought

John Dewey (1910) for example, presented his own model as an outgrowth of his "complete act of thought" philosophy. Dewey's learning cycle presumes that the teacher takes an active role in recognizing and developing the experiences of the learner who progresses through a series of processes to create new knowledge.

Dewey's steps for continuous learning include:

- Sense a perplexing situation,
- Clarify the problem,
- Formulate a hypothesis,
- Test the hypothesis,
- Revise tests, and
- Act on solutions.

The learner is central to this process while the teacher serves in the role of a "more knowledgeable other" and facilitator of learning (Dewey, 1938/1997).

Experiential Learning Cycles

A number of researchers have expanded upon Dewey's work, creating Experiential Learning Cycles (ELCs) to describe the learning process (Kolb, 1984; Honey & Mumford, 1982). These learning cycles depict learning as a process rather than an outcome. ELCs incorporate Dewey's foundational belief that learning is a complex process that results from interactions among the learner, her environment, and the experiences, perceptions, and feelings the learner brings to the task at hand. Such ELCs are designed to help teachers structure learning projects that take into account the experiences of the individual learner and include processes that support children's educational development.

Learning Network© Teaching-Learning Cycle

Some teaching-learning cycles center on the steps the teacher takes to support children in their learning. These models are predicated on the belief that the teacher must know the learner and her level of understanding in order to create appropriate instruction. One such model, based on Vygotsky's (1978) concept of *zone of proximal development* (ZPD), is presented in the teaching-learning cycle created by Richard Owens Learning Network (Herzog, 1997). This model relies on a cycle that has four essential elements: assessment, evaluation, planning, and teaching. The cycle defines the steps the teacher takes to ensure the children's learning is successful. Through assessment and evaluation the teacher is able to provide the child with appropriate scaffolding until the child masters the concepts the teacher is presenting. This is an interesting paradigm shift from models that focus on the progressive steps that the child takes to assimilate new information.

Instead, the teacher selects a goal, assesses the child's mastery level in association with that goal, and plans instruction to support the child in attaining higher levels of success.

The Five-E Model

Another popular model depicting the learning cycle is the "Five-E Learning Cycle." Teachers often use this model as a tool for designing science instruction, as it promotes inquiry-based learning. Karplus and Thier (1967) first proposed the model, and it was expanded upon by Roger Bybee, principal investigator of the Biological Science Curriculum Study team (BSCS, 2001). The Five-E model describes teaching and learning as a five-stage process:

- Engaging,
- Exploring,
- Explaining,
- Elaborating, and
- Evaluating.

The Five-E model particularly supports teaching practices based on constructivist philosophy. The Five-E model describes the processes children use as they build their understanding about a particular problem. When children are curious about an idea or concept, they *engage* in the process. As they begin interacting with the materials and working together with their classmates, they move into the *exploration* phase. Children develop and clarify their understandings as they articulate them during the *explanation* phase. During this time, the children's vocabulary expands in a meaningful way (rather than through looking words up in a dictionary or hearing the teacher provide definitions). In stage four, *elaboration*, children consider the applications of their learning and the implications for their own experience in the world. *Evaluation* takes place throughout the discourse. It is ongoing and cyclical with questions leading not only to answers but also to more hypotheses.

Inquiry-based Learning

Inquiry-based learning relies upon the concept that children make connections between their prior knowledge and new stimuli. In this approach to teaching and learning, teachers support children in gathering, organizing, and evaluating information. Teachers design instruction to encourage the generalization of ideas and concepts, a process that creates a foundation for further study. Unlike the circular process of Kolb and Fry (1975), this model is progressive in design, with each stage building upon the previous one.

Four-Stage Teaching and Learning Cycle

Bredekamp and Rosegrant (1992) describe the teaching-learning process in terms of four progressing stages of learning: *awareness, exploration, inquiry,* and *utilization.*

Awareness
Children approach new learning from an *awareness* stage. At this level, the child is exposed to concepts and ideas. The teacher observes the children in her class to determine their interests and background knowledge. Talking with children about activities of daily living cultivates *awareness.* These conversations expand not only the children's concepts but also increase oral language development and interest. In this way the teacher develops instructional opportunities that are based in common understandings and provides materials and activities that support engagement. This learning stage helps create context for learning.

Exploration
During the next level of the cycle, *exploration,* children are curious and want to independently investigate the materials or concepts presented to them. Observing, collecting information, constructing personal understanding, and creating meaning are activities associated with this level of learning. At this stage, children investigate things of interest to them by using ideas or materials in unconventional—yet personally meaningful—ways.

Inquiry
When children become comfortable with the materials and vocabulary associated with a particular material or concept, they are free to enter the inquiry phase of the

teaching-learning cycle. Here the teacher can present a problem for children to solve. During the process, the child begins to compare her learning with that of others. Through careful observation, the teacher can determine when a child is ready to apply conventional strategies to master an idea or task. Key to supporting the children at this level is helping them make connections between the task at hand and their previous learning.

Utilization

Finally, when children have acquired a new skill, they are anxious to apply it in an authentic context. The *utilization* stage of the teaching-learning cycle focuses on the functionality of a skill. Through continued usage, children become more adept at using their skills across a variety of environments. The role of the teacher shifts to providing meaningful contexts for children to use and solidify their new learning.

Summary

A host of teaching-learning cycles are available for the practitioner to consider as a framework for instruction. In fact, many states and school districts are constructing their own models and maintain an expectation that their teachers will follow those models for planning and for instruction. Most models of the teaching-learning cycle capture the notion that children need support as they take on and process new learning. The reflective teacher will use a variety of tools to provide that support. The classroom environment can be one of these teaching tools.

For the teachers of young children, the key concept to remember is that learning (and teaching) is a dynamic process and it is the learner who sits at the center of that process. The role of the teacher becomes one of facilitating the learning and designing the environment in order to support the learning process for all children. What physical design supports the teaching-learning cycle? What social-emotional climate encourages children to move through the steps of the learning cycle? What experiences should be planned to foster children's engagement in the learning process? What opportunities do children need in order to engage in higher levels of understanding? How do teachers use the learning environment as a teaching tool in this process? Research about best practices in combination with reflection will guide the thoughtful practitioner to discover the answers to these questions.

Best Practices: Foundations for Structuring the Classroom Environment

Brain-based Research

The learning environment must enhance learning, not impede it. The foundational support for a re-design of the learning environment is found in recent brain-based research. During the 1990s, which was declared the "Decade of the Brain," researchers did important work to help explore the importance of environment on the brain, how a child's brain develops and its relationship to learning.

Dr. Marian Diamond—a neuroscientist and researcher from the University of California at Berkeley—and her colleagues did pioneering work with laboratory rats in the 1950s and found that positive physiological changes in rat brains occurred when they were stimulated with an enriched environment (Diamond, Krech, & Rosenweig, 1964). Additionally, recent studies of the human brain have observed dendrite growth as a result of stimulation provided in enriched environments. We learn from Diamond's initial research, and research following hers, that stimulation from enriched experiences and environments promotes positive brain development (Diamond & Hopson, 1998; Kempermann, Kuhn & Gage, 1997). The human brain is highly plastic and constantly changing, especially during the critical years of early childhood development, birth through age eight. Stimulating, enriched environments can grow dendrites while dull or unchallenging environments can impede brain development or growth.

Leslie Hart (1998) builds a bridge between theory and pracice by describing the impact that emotions and the absence of threat can play in the creation of a positive learning climate for children. An absence of threat enhances children's learning. Hart describes a body-brain partnership—one that engages the learner physically in the learning process—as happening within an emotionally safe and supportive classroom environment. This means an environment that promotes a sense of community, involves learning content and mastery, and includes real-world application as the goal. Hart believes the physical environment of our schools should be: 1) healthful, clean, and well-lighted; 2) uncluttered; 3) well laid out for multiple uses; 4) pleasant smelling; 5) aesthetically pleasing with calm colors, plants, and music; and 6) supplied with multiple resources to be used for topics of study (Hart, 1998).

Work by Eric Jensen connects research with teaching strategies in order to have a positive impact on teaching and learning in schools. "Learners in positive, joyful environments are likely to experience enhanced learning, memory, and feelings of self-esteem" (Jensen, 2000, p. 109). Teachers have a responsibility as facilitators of learning to create a positive physical and psychological environment. Jensen (2000) identifies the following environmental influences as important to consider when planning the physical classroom environment: "seating options, manipulatives, music, color, peripherals, plants, lighting, aromas, room arrangement, concrete objects, and ionization" (p. 63).

In addition to knowledge about how the brain receives and processes information, teachers must recognize the developmental processes of the learner and the role of experience in learning. Developmentally appropriate practice works in concert with the findings of research about the brain.

Developmentally Appropriate Practice

Bredekamp & Copple (1997) define developmentally appropriate practices as practices that result from decisions about the well-being and education of children which are based on at least three important kinds of information or knowledge:

1. What is known about child development and learning—knowledge of age-related human characteristics that permits general predictions within an age range about what activities, materials, interactions or experiences will be safe, healthy, interesting, achievable, and also challenging to children.
2. What is known about the strengths, interests, and needs of each individual child in the group so as to be able to adapt for and be responsive to individual variation.
3. Knowledge of the social and cultural contexts in which children live to ensure that learning experiences are meaningful, relevant, and respectful for the participating children and their families (pp. 8–9).

It is crucial to keep these points in mind when educating young children. Integration of the curriculum and meaningful learning are examples of developmentally appropriate practice in the primary setting. School should be fun for children of all ages, especially during the early years of schooling, as this sets the stage for future learning. If learning is fun and meaningful, then children develop a love of learning and a desire to know, think, and understand. The teacher has a significant role to play in helping children develop joy in the learning process. According to Copple & Bredekamp (2009), the teacher plays a key role by, (1) creating a caring community of learners, (2) teaching to enhance development and learning, (3) planning curriculum to achieve important goals, (4) assessing children's development and learning, and (5) establishing reciprocal relationships with families (p.34). The physical classroom environment is the foundation on which the teacher builds this structure.

The classroom environment is a tool for teacher and child. It should be warm and inviting as well as healthy and safe. The environment must be clean and contain materials safe for children to use. Ensure that all classroom furnishings are stable and well maintained. If the children are proud of their classroom, it will encourage them to become responsible learners and caretakers of their environment.

When organizing a classroom space, have routines and procedures in mind for efficient and proper use by children. The space should be divided into areas for large group meetings, small group instruction, collaborative learning, and exploration of concepts, using a variety of materials for both individuals and small groups. Flexible use of space is critical. Organization of the classroom should allow children to explore, interact, and become involved in learning.

It is important to include time and space for reflection in the learning process. As children engage in active exploration of concepts, they learn that it is "okay" and safe to make mistakes. Children learn from their own experiences and the experiences of others in the learning community as they share ideas, perceptions, and the work they have accomplished (Dewey, 1938/1997). By working individually and with others, the child begins to value her own "think time" and to understand the critical role this reflection plays in the learning process.

Also important is the use of peripherals. Peripherals are artifacts created during the learning process that are then placed around the classroom to reflect and extend the learning. They are evidence of learning and are connected to current topics of study. Peripherals often are child-generated and support their understanding. They are tools for continuous learning. Be careful that the environment is not over-stimulating or overly colorful, and that commercial materials not representative of the learning taking place are kept to a minimum. The learning of the class as a whole and individuals within the class community should be apparent for all to see.

Constructivism

In the constructivist, learner-centered classroom, teachers focus on promoting the learning process and developing children's sense of individual and group worth. According to Brooks & Brooks (2001), there are 12 essential components to constructivist teaching:

1. Encouragement and acceptance of student autonomy and initiative.
2. Use of raw data and primary sources along with manipulative, interactive, and physical materials.
3. Use of cognitive terminology such as "classify," "analyze," "predict," and "create."
4. Allowing student responses to drive lessons, shift instructional strategies, and alter content.
5. Inquiring about students' understanding of concepts before teachers share their own understanding of those concepts.
6. Encouraging students to engage in dialogue, both with the teacher and with one another.
7. Encouraging student inquiry by asking thoughtful, open-ended questions and encouraging students to ask questions of each other.
8. Seeking elaboration of students' initial responses.
9. Engaging students in experiences that might engender contradictions to their initial hypotheses and then encouraging discussion.
10. Allowing wait time after posing questions.
11. Providing time for students to construct relationships and create metaphors.
12. Nurturing students' natural curiosity through frequent use of the learning cycle model (pps. 103–118).

A constructivist environment is learner-centered (Henson, 2003) and considers both the developmental stage of the child and the individuality of the process. In these classrooms children are encouraged to create their own schemas for understanding. Teachers also provide context for children as they construct the neural networks associated with logical-mathematical, physical, conventional, and social learning (DeVries & Kamii, 1980).

Teachers in the constructivist classroom recognize that learning is a social process. A climate of respect is an integral part of the teaching-learning process. In the social context, children experiment and cooperate with one another while exploring their interests (DeVries, Hildebrandt, Edmiaston, & Sales, 2002). The teacher creates opportunities and guides these explorations toward meaningful learning. Through an interactive and dynamic learning process, children develop the higher-level thinking skills they need to ask questions about the world around them, as well as the associated strategies necessary to find answers to those questions.

The constructivist environment looks, sounds, and feels different from the traditional classroom. Careful design of the environment is vital to create a successful learner-centered classroom. The pedagogy and environment that support teaching and learning lie on a continuum, with the traditional classroom on the left, constructivist classroom on the right and the non-traditional falling in between. The constructivist classroom supports distinct types of learning: meaningful learning, social learning, purposeful learning, responsible learning, continuous learning, and inquiry-based learning. Teachers can move from traditional classroom design to non-traditional and, ultimately, constructivist classroom design and pedagogy by using professional development and reflection to expand their understanding of learning and the role of the classroom environment as a major teaching tool.

Pedagogy and Environments of Traditional and Constructivist Classrooms: Types of Learning

Meaningful Learning

A classroom's physical environment tells a story about the type of learning that takes place in that classroom. The environment that leads to meaningful learning is warm and inviting. It is a healthy classroom. This classroom is clean and well maintained. The temperature is controlled. There is a water source for rehydration, and snacks are available throughout the learning day. In the healthy classroom, lighting is varied, with natural light being an important dimension for the room. (This type of lighting contrasts dramatically with lighting in a traditional classroom, where light comes primarily from overhead fixtures.) The healthy classroom is stimulating, accommodating to the learners, and comfortable. It is welcoming, with a backdrop of calming colors, and includes plants and music. It is inviting, and it projects a sense of community. Incorporating these Foundational Elements for Physically and Emotionally Safe Classrooms supports children in their engagement in *meaningful learning*.

Social Learning

Social learning is an integral part of the constructivist learning environment. The more traditional classroom is structured so that children do more learning in isolation. These traditional structures may include rows of desks for the children and a teacher desk or podium at the front and center of the classroom. There is a schedule, and all children work individually on the same tasks at the same time. The teacher provides materials to the children as they are needed to complete specific tasks. These structures highlight that the teacher controls the learning and limits movement and social interaction in the classroom. In the constructivist classroom, by contrast, learning occurs through social interaction.

To encourage social learning, the teacher who implements constructivist strategies creates a physical design that supports social interaction. There are defined learning spaces for individual, collaborative, and whole group work.

The Classroom Is Arranged for Learning and Positive Learning Interactions.
Arrangement of furniture should allow for a variety of social learning opportunities throughout the day. It should offer easy identification of tables, seating choices, and spaces for individual work, small group work, large group work, and gathering. The variety of learning spaces with multiple uses offers children opportunities to construct knowledge actively instead of passively receiving knowledge.

Purposeful Learning

It is simple to identify a classroom designed for *purposeful learning.* In constructivist classrooms, spaces and materials call children to engage in the process of learning. Such classrooms frequently integrate the concepts from a variety of subject areas (reading, writing, science, social studies, and math). The process is just as important, if not more important, than the product. In contrast, a more traditional classroom focuses primarily on isolated skill development and final products. Children work independently with worksheets and multiple textbooks while teachers teach subjects independent of one another.

The Organized Classroom Physically Arranged for Focused Learning will contain learning centers or stations housing a variety of materials. These are key components for creating constructivist environments and give children the opportunity to focus on the process of learning. Learning centers and carpeted areas enhance the learning space. Some surfaces are soft and some are hard in order to increase the functionality of the space. Children move through the room from one learning area to another based on their interests as well as the design of the learning. The room arrangement encourages both active and quiet learning. Throughout the room there are materials organized and available for exploration in clearly defined learning spaces. Children know their choices and the specific purposes of the learning spaces in the room.

Personal spaces for storage, areas for display of the children's work, along with organized and flexible teacher space, lead children to *purposeful learning*.

Responsible Learning

Children develop real-life skills as they engage in learning in classrooms that reflect a sense of community. In constructivist classrooms, children take ownership for their own learning and work together with the teacher to accomplish learning goals. The classroom must be organized in order for children to develop skills for *responsible learning*. In traditional classrooms, children are not responsible for their own learning; textbooks drive the teaching and learning processes. In these more traditional educational settings, the commercially purchased materials, worksheets, and textbooks are tools for learning. Typically, an overabundance of these materials and peripherals consume the learning space. The teacher is responsible for determining which materials the children will use, when the children will use these materials, as well as determining procedures and routines for using them without input from children.

Furthermore, in traditional classrooms, there is a focus on rules designed to maintain order. This discourages *responsible learning,* because the teacher controls the order of the clasroom. As a result, children learn in isolation. Children are expected to complete their lessons and assignments without much, if any, social interaction. These classrooms often implement systems of rewards and punishment (Jonassen, 1991) that reward individual children for appropriate behaviors. Consequences for inappropriate behaviors generally become more severe as those behaviors persist, indicating the teacher's belief that it is possible to curtail such behavior when the consequence is severe enough.

The constructivist approach encourages children to be responsible for their own learning. The design of the classroom supports children as they access and use the available resources. This requires a thoughtfully organized classroom.

Organize Materials in the Classroom to Promote Engagement in Learning:
This will include de-cluttering the environment, organizing materials so children can use those materials as tools in the learning process, arranging materials so they are accessible, and working with the children to develop procedures and routines that promote responsibility among the children. In *responsible learning* classrooms, teachers recognize that learning is social. They incorporate structures that support the development of a learning community.

Positive character development and respect for individual differences are concepts a teacher can foster through classroom conversations and procedures. This approach encourages children to help one another through the learning process and teaches them how to work together to be productive. It makes materials accessible to the children, while individual plans and class agendas guide the work of the day. This environment helps to highlight children's understanding of their roles as members of a group and their responsibility for self-management. Children take ownership for their own learning and work together with the teacher to accomplish individual learning goals. The constructivist classroom helps children develop into responsible learners who have effective self-regulation skills (Bronson, 2000).

Continuous Learning

Classroom Peripherals Represent the Learning Process and Learning Projects and indicate whether a classroom supports *continuous learning*. Peripherals in the constructivist classroom represent learning, are authentic, and document the learning process. In traditional classrooms, however, peripherals consist mostly of commercially produced posters placed around the room to reinforce skill development. The room lacks photographs of the actual learning process, artifacts that children create during the learning process, children's portfolios, and child-created representations of the knowledge and skills they are developing. In the traditional classroom the focus is on outcomes; peripherals include posting of final tests, worksheets, and products that all look the same.

Peripherals in the child-centered classroom, however, document the progress of children engaged in active, *continuous learning*. Such peripherals serve as evidence that children are tapping into prior knowledge, planning, and investigating. Peripherals can be a variety of artifacts created by children that serve as useful, formative assessments. The skilled educator uses these peripherals to assess, plan, evaluate, and drive instruction to ensure every learner's continuous progress (Herzog, 1997).

Reflection is a key component of *continuous learning*. Constructivist classrooms place a high value on collaborative engagement (Dangel, Guyton, & McIntyre, 2003) where talk is tri-dimensional: child-to-child; child-to-teacher; and teacher-to-child. These classrooms have a conversational tone, center on the learning process, and reflect the subject under investigation. The teacher serves as only one participant in the dialogue. Phrases such as "I'm wondering" and "Tell me about your thinking" are an integral part of the discourse and reflection process. Peripherals capture this process and document ongoing explorations that result from this dialogue (Forman & Fyfe, 1998).

Inquiry-based Learning

An inquiry-based classroom emphasizes in-depth study and problem-solving. This high-level learning is one of the goals of the constructivist ***Classroom Ready for In-depth Study.*** In traditional classrooms, by contrast, the teacher is the transmitter of knowledge (Gardner, 1991). The teacher directs instruction and the talk is primarily from teacher to child. This aspect of the traditional classroom arises from the need to maintain order. When children interact with one another, traditional classroom thinking assumes the teacher does not have the attention of the children. If the teacher is not the transmitter of knowledge, the reasoning goes, the children cannot be acquiring the skills they need to learn.

In a traditional design, the accumulation of knowledge is central to the instructional process. It discourages the exploration of ideas and concepts because the teacher focuses on "covering" the day's necessary content. This values the single "right" answer over a broader exploration of ideas; when children submit a correct answer, they are able to move to the next skill set. The traditional classroom teacher designs instruction that moves from "parts" to "whole." In order to accomplish this progression, the teacher must present textbooks, packets, worksheets, and repetitive tasks in a particular sequence. This leads to children acquiring discrete pieces of information, and frequently encourages memorization. Prepared visuals transmit fixed ideas, as contrasted with a display of children's work, which documents the children's learning. In the traditional classroom, the focus in on the product.

In the constructivist classroom, the learner is central to the learning; children inquire and explore rather than memorize and repeat. Children enjoy an active interaction with learning materials and processes. The environment is rich, including computers, research materials, and resources. Peripherals depict evidence of planning and collaboration. Visible throughout the classroom are graphic organizers, schedules that allow adequate time for in-depth exploration, and evidence of sharing ideas and findings. It is easy to observe the various stages of the learning cycle.

The constructivist classroom provides children with an emotionally safe environment, a crucial element in any child's educational development. Such a space helps children learn to value the process of learning, and it allows children to construct their own knowledge through the exploration of ideas. A typical example of this kind of exploration includes "project work that develops layers of content knowledge and allows different levels of engagement and interaction" (Dangel et al, 2003, p. 240). The inquiry-based environment encourages children to take risks by sharing their ideas openly with one another. This results in quality conversations between children; as a result, the children develop ideas that transmit and internalize learning.

The constructivist classroom has a curricular design that is typically experiential, so that learning moves from "whole" to "parts." The focus is on the process of learning. The result is an incorporation of children's exploration and authentic experiences into the teaching-learning cycle. There are blocks of time scheduled for child-driven discovery, the intention being that in this way the children develop a continual and self-sustained interest in learning (Rushton and Larkin, 2001). Children work through the curriculum in ways that allow them to make connections through multiple experiences over time.

When developing a child-centered classroom design, the thoughtful practitioner should consider the following ideas as they relate to the children: *meaningful learning*, *social learning*, *purposeful learning*, *responsible learning*, *continuous learning,* and *inquiry-based learning*. The *Primary Educator's Environment Checklist* in Chapter 10 can serve as a guide to assess and to create the kind of educational environment described above. The process of reflection and change begins with analyzing the environment and it leads to thinking about how pedagogy can focus on the needs of the individual child as well as the group.

The ***Pedagogy and Environment of Traditional and Constructivist Classrooms*** table below highlights some of the differences between traditional and constructivist classrooms in relation to the environment's physical design and pedagogy. Traditional classroom environments are mostly teacher-centered, constructivist classrooms are more child-centered, with non-traditional environments situated in between the two.

Table II | Pedagogy and Environment of Traditional and Constructivist Classrooms

Six crucial educational categories emerge in the constructivist columns of this table: Meaningful Learning, Social Learning, Purposeful Learning, Responsible Learning, Continuous Learning, and Inquiry-based Learning. In order to move from a traditional to non-traditional or constructivist classroom design and pedagogy, it is important to review and update the educational environment. Educators can observe children acquiring skills in these six categories of learning. Promoting these six learning categories through constructivist-based classroom arrangement and pedagogy will help change the face of what education looks like, feels like, and is for elementary-aged children.

Traditional	Constructivist
Pedagogy—Children are passive recipients of knowledge. **Environment**—sterile, cold, desks in rows, teacher's desk front and center, textbooks	**Pedagogy**—Children are active constructors of knowledge. **Environment**—warm, inviting, learning topic apparent, daily agendas, knowledge of children present, group discussion areas, hands-on materials, centers and work stations, evidence connecting skills to real life, problem-solving evidence—promotes **Meaningful Learning**
Pedagogy—Learning occurs as children work independently on assignments. **Environment**—children at desks working independently, teacher directs whole group lecture	**Pedagogy**—Learning occurs through social interaction. **Environment**—defined learning spaces for individual, collaborative, and whole group work; class meeting area; work space for teacher-guided instruction with small groups—promotes **Social Learning**
Pedagogy—Classroom focus is primarily on isolated skills and final products. **Environment**—children at desks, multiple worksheets, multiple textbooks, teaching of subject areas independent of one another	**Pedagogy**—Focus is on process as well as product. **Environment**—children choose work stations or centers, materials for exploration and interactive learning, organized environment allows children to access and use materials—promotes **Purposeful Learning**
Pedagogy—Textbooks drive the curriculum. **Environment**—desks, textbooks, worksheets, environments full of commercially purchased materials that are over stimulating, teacher responsible for materials, procedures and communication	**Pedagogy**—Hands-on materials, real-life learning, technology, and answering questions through research drive the learning process. **Environment**—accessible and organized materials, de-cluttered environments, procedures and communication routines in place to promote children's responsibility—promotes **Responsible Learning**
Pedagogy—Assessment focus is on grades and primarily summative; reflection is not part of the learning process. **Environment**—peripherals include posting of completed worksheets, tests, final products, and final grades	**Pedagogy**—Assessment is formative and focus is on continuous progress; reflection is a key component in the continuous cycle of teaching and learning. **Environment**—peripherals include evidence of tapping into prior knowledge, planning, elaboration, and investigation; collection of multiple artifacts used to assess, plan, evaluate continuously—promotes **Continuous Learning**
Pedagogy—Emphasis is on acquiring facts. **Environment**—large group instruction, factual recall on tests, schedules that depict teaching in isolation without adequate time for exploration	**Pedagogy**—Emphasis is on in-depth study and problem-solving. **Environment**—computers and research materials, peripherals that are evidence of planning, use of graphic organizers, schedules that allow for adequate time for in-depth exploration and sharing or ideas and findings—promotes **Inquiry-based Learning**

© Evanshen

A Room to Learn

Foundational Elements for Physically and Emotionally Safe Classrooms:
The Healthy Classroom

Use the *Primary Educator's Environment Checklist* (see page 181) to assess classroom learning environments and examine the following topics: whether the classroom is **Well-Maintained**, with attention to cleanliness and safety; **Lighting**, including natural and varied sources; and **Nourishment**, including providing water and healthy snacks. These foundational elements, along with those found in Chapter Four, *Foundational Elements for Physically and Emotionally Safe Classrooms: The Welcoming Classroom*, contribute to the successful design of a physically and emotionally safe classroom where meaningful learning can occur. Are there structures in place to meet children's physiological and safety needs (Maslow, 1943)?

The Well-Maintained Classroom

The classroom environment is one of the primary foundations for children's learning. As Leslie Hart (1998) states, "Learning is enhanced when, in addition to ensuring an absence of threat, the body-brain partnership has a supportive physical environment and meaningful curriculum content" (p. 206). Children who feel safe and cared for are more ready to learn. The appearance of a classroom speaks volumes to children, so teachers must design their classrooms to support children's sense of well-being. What do children see when they walk into their learning environment? Children in a teacher's care deserve an environment that not only is supportive of their learning, but also is well-maintained, safe, and meets their basic needs.

"Before" Photos

When assessing classrooms, we find that teachers often neglect basic safety issues. With the increase of electronic devices in education, the treatment of electrical cords becomes an issue associated with safety. These pictures capture what happens when the omnipresent cords are not strategically considered.

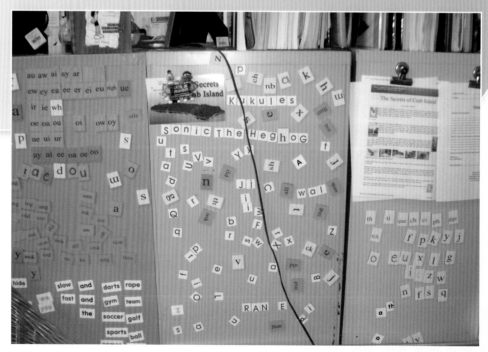

Notice how the children's reading area is next to two potential health issues, a trash can and a dusty heating vent.

Always maintain free access through the doorway. Furniture constricts this exit, creating a safety hazard.

Key Points

- Consider safety hazards. Monitor electrical equipment to make certain that cords are well-maintained and out of children's reach.
- Children are quick to detect odors. The olfactory portions of our brains have receptors for endorphins, which increase our sense of well-being. Research (Dhong, Chung, & Doty, 1999; Pauli, Bourne, Diekmann, & Birbaumer, 1999; Herz, 2009) shows a link between associative memory and smells.
- The classroom should be well-ventilated and stay at a temperature of approximately 70° F (Jensen, 2000).

Suggestions

- To keep electrical cords out of children's reach, you can use flexible tubing. Do not overload power strips and keep cords away from work areas and walkways.
- Furniture should be well-maintained. Ensure furniture is free from splinters and rough edges. Repurpose, repair, or discard older furniture. Assess classroom furniture. Should it be discarded, or does it just need a fresh coat of paint? Make certain to use non-toxic materials when repairing and updating furniture.
- Doorways should be free of furniture and clutter. There should be clear access to the doorway. This serves as a safety feature and also creates a welcoming and inviting entrance to the room.
- A classroom needs to be maintained well. Clean thoroughly and regularly.
- If posting items on a wall, ensure that they are fastened securely. Posters, pictures, and children's work flapping in the wind can make a classroom look cluttered, can distract children, and often catch dust.
- Involve the children in maintaining the cleanliness and organization of the classroom. Use consistent procedures for clean-up, and make this a part of the daily routine.
- Think about the possibility of cross-contamination. Trash cans should be easily accessible to children; however, it is unsanitary to place trash cans in the children's work areas.

- Create personal spaces for children's belongings. This will provide children with a sense of security and independence. Additionally, creating these personal spaces can have the added benefit of keeping articles of clothing off the floor in the coat closet, and minimizing contagious health risks (such as lice).

- The impact of aromas on learning is being studied. In one study, introducing lemon essential oils to the classroom environment was positively related to attention and cognition (Akpinar, 2005). Jenson (2003) suggests experimenting with natural scents such as peppermint, vanilla, cinnamon, lemon, lavender, and chamomile. **Note**: Do not use any flammable materials, such as candles, to achieve this effect. Likewise, spraying air fresheners is not an adequate substitute for natural scents. Also, keep in mind that some children have allergies.

- Live plants can serve as natural air filters (Wolverton, Johnson, & Bounds, 1989). Artificial plants can make a classroom harder to maintain because they attract dirt and are difficult to clean. (See more about the importance of plants in Chapter 4.)

- All primary classrooms should have carpeted areas. Low pile and inexpensive area carpets allow for easy replacement. Carpets can harbor allergens, and frequent cleaning is not an option in most schools. For this reason, replaceable carpets are preferable.

"After" Photos

Electrical cords from the light and the CD player are tucked behind the shelving. This reduces the chance that the children will become entangled in the cords.

This classroom has a carpeted area for large group gatherings. It is low pile and easy to clean. Note the cleanliness of the environment for group meetings.

Children's personal belongings are stored in individual bags that hang from hooks. These bags can be made for you or can be purchased from a laundry supply business.

Lighting

Lighting is an important component of the healthy classroom (Jensen, 2003). Lighting is a key ingredient for setting the tone for learning. Teachers can alter the learning environment by using a variety of lighting sources (including using the natural light available through classroom windows). Well-placed lighting can create interest, define classroom centers, and create a home-like environment. Poor lighting, on the other hand, can detract from learning and disengage children from the learning process.

"Before" Photos

In this classroom the blinds are closed and commercially prepared posters are attached to them, blocking out natural light.

Fluorescent lighting can make the environment feel sterile.

Natural Light and Varied Lighting

Key Points

- Classrooms that have access to natural light should take advantage of it. Natural lighting "brings the outside in." This is especially important since children spend less and less time outdoors. In his research, Wayne London demonstrated the positive impact of light on children's performance. He found that children in brightly lit classrooms miss fewer days of school, thereby increasing their opportunity to learn (as cited in Jensen, 2000).
- Natural light covers the full range of the light spectrum and helps us maintain natural biological rhythms. Unlike fluorescent lighting, there is no oscillation/flicker of natural light, a characteristic associated with adverse reactions in many children (Irlen, 1991; Jensen, 2003; Wilkins, Nimmo-Smith, Slater, & Bedocs, 1989).
- There is a documented connection between higher levels of natural lighting and improved performance (Hathaway, Hargreaves, Thompson, & Novitsky, 1992; Heschong Mahone Group, 1999; Dunn, Krimsky, Murray, & Quinn, 1985).
- Using different types of lighting helps define learning areas in the classroom and makes the atmosphere more comfortable and homelike. Purposeful placement of lighting, however, is important. Scattering lamps around a classroom at random provides a variety of lighting; nevertheless, it does not serve to focus children's attention on learning.
- Isbell and Exelby (2001) suggest exchanging the cool, white fluorescent lights found in many classrooms with full-spectrum tubes.

Natural Lighting: Suggestions

- Replace tattered or troublesome window shades. Better options include blinds and curtains. Lightweight curtains hanging on tension rods are relatively easy to install and maintain.
- If the sun shines directly into children's eyes, adjust blinds so that light can still filter into the room. Unfiltered light that causes a glare can reduce children's attention on the task at hand. If possible, avoid closing the blinds altogether.
- Consider using sheer curtains as a filter for intense light. Hang them using a tension rod for ease in opening and closing. Sheer curtains are especially useful in combination with blinds (see photo on page 49).
- If windows have window treatments, determine how to arrange them to allow for maximum lighting. Window treatments should have multiple functions, including sound absorption, light management, and aesthetic properties.

- Window treatments should be neutral in color. Bold patterns and bright colors detract from the impact of the natural light from the windows.
- Revitalize old lamps found in attics, garage sales, and secondhand shops by adding new, neutral-toned shades.
- If possible, try turning off all lights so the classroom is illuminated primarily by natural light during some parts of the day.
- Consider the placement of learning centers and stations. For example, it is best not to place computers under a window that receives direct sunlight. This scenario can create a glare and impact children's ability to see the computer screen easily.
- Add mirrors to reflect natural light and make spaces appear larger (Isbell & Exelby, 2001).

Varied Lighting: Suggestions
- Strategic placement of lamps is important. Putting a lamp at a learning center, for example, helps define that space as a learning center or station. Using a table lamp not only provides for more light, but also "spotlights" the materials available for children to use.
- Consider child safety when determining how to arrange lights' power cords.
- Create interest by using a variety of lighting sources throughout the room.
- Provide choices of high-light and low-light areas. Children will naturally move to the space that is illuminated according to their light preference or learning style (Dunn, Dunn, & Perrin, 1994).
- Never place a lamp near a source of water.

"After" Photos

Using curtains in combination with window blinds allows for flexibility in controlling light. Curtains also add softness to the room.

"After" Photos

Cork pads between windows can act as a sound absorption feature, while blinds control the flow of light. Notice how the trees outside the classroom add to the naturalistic appeal of the room.

A table lamp not only provides additional lighting but also "spotlights" the materials. Adding a table lamp turns a chair into a quiet reading space.

This teacher station is in a corner of a classroom. The teacher uses this area for small group instruction. Notice how the light highlights the instructional focus on the bulletin board.

Nourishment

Good nutrition not only affects children's physical health, but also helps promote efficient brain function. In their work, Jensen (2000), Hart (1998), Levine & Coe (1989), and Bernath & Masi (2006) discuss the role of food and water and their importance for learning. However, the impact of nutrition throughout the day is one aspect of the learning environment that primary grade educators frequently neglect. The neurons in the brain rely upon glucose, oxygen, and water for optimal functioning. Physically speaking, when the brain is "satisfied" with its access to these ingredients, it is much more able to focus on learning. Emotionally, children who work and play in an environment that has water and nutritious snacks readily available are able to concentrate on more challenging tasks because they perceive that their basic needs will be met (Jensen, 2000).

The importance of breakfast in providing glucose for boosting brain function led the federal government to expand its 1969 Free Lunch Program to offer breakfast for free and at reduced rates in public schools in 1975. Nutritional deficiencies are common in children. While classroom teachers cannot provide children with all their nutritional needs, providing children with access to brain-friendly foods and water can provide positive benefits in attention, focus, and perseverance in the classroom. Doing this in a safe and sanitary manner reinforces the message of a healthy environment.

Key Points

- According to the USDA, in 2008, 14.6% of the households in America were classified as "food insecure" (Nord, Andrews, and Carlson, 2009). Many children function at the "basic needs" level and come to school each day hungry. Others have nutritional deficiencies. Even children who do not fall into these categories can benefit by having a steady intake of brain-friendly fuel to support the brain.
- The brain consists of 80% water. Water is required for efficient neural connections and healthy brain activity. Water also keeps the lungs moist and enhances transfer of oxygen into the blood stream (Sousa, 2001).

Suggestions

- Know children's medical needs. Many children have allergies to a variety of foods. Post food allergens in general terms in a conspicuous place in your room. For example, "No Peanut Products in This Classroom." It is inappropriate, however, to identify publicly a particular child as having a food allergy. Notify those who provide snacks (frequently parents and family members) about products they should avoid sending to school with their children.
- Healthy snacks can include fruits, vegetables, cheese, sunflower seeds, raisins, and yogurt.
- When designing procedures for your children, consider these questions: How will children access water for rehydration? What is the best design to ensure that snack time is sanitary? What is the safest way to make snacks available for the children?
- Consider how the smells of snacks can contribute to children's attention. The simple act of cutting oranges into wedges or eating peppermint can release scents into the room that impact attentional states (Jenson, 2000).
- Provide a basket of healthy, pre-packaged snacks. Develop procedures with children to encourage responsible snacking throughout the day, or schedule snack times into the morning and afternoon routines. Some teachers require both morning and afternoon snacks and pair the snacks with choice activities for the children to complete each morning and afternoon. An example of such a pairing is a "Brain Booster" snack and activity. Children take their snack from the Brain Booster basket at any point during this time and then mark the

activity "complete" on their personal agendas before going on to explore the learning centers. Other teachers choose to put children into learning groups and rotate them through morning and afternoon centers. Each learning group eats its snack in the classroom "restaurant" in a designated order. Although this procedure limits the freedom each learner has to choose when to eat snack, it does improve the sanitary conditions of the classroom.

- Design methods of distributing snacks and water that will not interrupt the instructional components of the classroom. Create these procedures with the children and implement them consistently. Plan these procedures according to the maturity of the children, and be sure to include ideas for clean-up after snack times. Younger children may manage cups with lids or small disposable cups more easily than other types of beverage containers.

- Pure water is the best product for rehydration. Providing children frequent access to water ensures that their brains and bodies stay hydrated. Choose from a variety of options for providing water, depending on your particular circumstances. For example, children can bring their own filled water bottles to school each day. Washable cups with lids are an option, especially when these cups have the children's names printed on them in permanent marker. Parents and family members may want to donate recyclable bottles of water. Some classrooms have water fountains in them, though it is better not to rely on a water fountain in the hall outside the classroom as the main source of water for the children. Having to send the children outside the classroom for water is disruptive to children's learning.

- Teaching children about proper nutrition and the importance of water is valuable for their independent understanding about healthy life habits. Educating parents and family members about the important role water and hydration play in their children's learning is also valuable, especially if you are asking parents and family members to provide bottled water or refillable water containers for the children.

- It is not uncommon for children to drink far more water than is necessary when "free water" is first available. This novelty wears off quickly, and the children's bodies begin to tell them when they need water. Nevertheless, during the initial stages of implementing hydration activities into the classroom, frequent trips to the bathroom are inevitable. Plan for this.

"After" Photos

Children in this classroom bring a variety of water bottles they can refill as necessary. To increase sanitary conditions, the children's names are written on their bottles in permanent marker.

It is important to have a designated place for snacks, specific procedures for eating snacks, and expectations for cleanliness when incorporating food and water into the daily routine.

Commentary

Teacher Comments

- My room was dark before I began this process because I kept my blinds closed. I thought the children would be distracted if they could see outside. There is a beautiful tree outside my window. I learned that, instead of the outside being a distraction, it seems to have a calming effect on the children (unless it's snowing!). My room is much more inviting with the additional natural light and the leafy green palette painted by the tree.

- Because of the direction of my classroom's windows, the sun shines directly into my children's eyes first thing in the morning. In the past, I closed my blinds to solve this problem, but I would forget to open them later in the morning. I now realize the importance of having natural light. I assign a child to be responsible for opening and closing the blinds. This not only promotes responsibility, but also teaches children about the healthy impact of sunlight.

- I am able to use natural light by using blinds and sheer curtains, reducing fluorescent lighting. I noticed it creates a calmer atmosphere more conducive to learning.

- I was afraid the children would need to be regulated in their access to snacks and water. I "let them go" the first two weeks and found that all but one self-regulated. I worked with the one child, recognizing that this was an opportunity to reinforce concepts of healthy choices. Food, and the meaning behind eating, is a complex issue for many children. My goal became helping them connect choices they made in the classroom to their daily lives.

- I do not like the mess associated with snacks. As a third-grade teacher, however, I understand that I can positively impact my children's learning by including nutritious snacks and water in the daily routine. I am working with my children to help them become responsible for cleaning up. We are eating more carrots and apples. Even the children see that they are easier to clean up and we all know how good they are for us.

Consultant Comments

- Cleaning house is the first step in the process of creating a healthy classroom. Ridding the classroom of furniture that is rarely used, stored materials that are seldom or never used, and items stored "just in case I need them" will start you on the journey to creating a healthy classroom.

- Using the Learning Style Model (Dunn, Dunn & Perrin, 1994) is helpful when considering children's preferences in relation to learning. Jensen's (2000, 1998, 1994) brain-based learning resources are helpful for gaining information on nutrition in an effort to boost attention and increase focus for learning.

Principal Comments

- I had a parent refuse to allow her child to be placed in Mrs. X's room because it was "too dark." I was surprised at her assertion that the teacher had no windows in the room and it "felt like a dungeon" because I knew that all our classrooms had a wall of windows. Mrs. X, however, kept her blinds closed at all times. The room did indeed appear dark and uninviting. Sometimes we forget that our children are not the only ones who react to the learning environment we establish; their parents are stakeholders in that environment as well.

- Our school is one of high poverty. We are working toward Universal Free Breakfast, a program offered by the federal government which allows all children in the school to start their day with a free, nutritious breakfast. We recognize that many children—those from homes of poverty as well as those from more affluent homes—come to school hungry. We believe that proactive efforts like this will help our children focus more on their learning and less on their physical needs.

Foundational Elements for Physically and Emotionally Safe Classrooms:
The Welcoming Classroom

Use the *Primary Educator's Environment Checklist* (see page 181) to assess classroom learning environments and examine the following topics: **Color** that is neutral and calming; whether a space is **Welcoming and Inviting** with music, plants, and home-like elements; and **Sense of Community,** highlighting photos and artifacts that demonstrate a caring climate. These foundational elements along with those found in Chapter Three, *The Foundational Elements for Physically and Emotionally Safe Classrooms: The Healthy Classroom,* contribute to the successful design of a physically and emotionally safe classroom where *meaningful learning* can occur.

Color

Color evokes emotion, contributes to mood, affects activity levels, and sets the tone for the classroom. Cool colors (blues and greens) and natural colors (beige and browns) contribute to the creation of a comfortable and relaxed environment (Hathaway, 1987). These are the colors that help create a backdrop for productive and focused learning.

"Before" Photos

In many classrooms colors are over-stimulating and potentially distracting for children. Other classrooms are colorless, with stark white surroundings.

A Room to Learn

Key Points

- Color can help to enhance moods and improve emotions and behavior. It may also impact cognition (Jensen, 2003).
- Warm colors (reds, oranges, and yellows) can increase blood pressure and active behavior (Taylor & Gousie, 1988).
- According to Olds (2001), "...inundation by bright primary colors can make children hyperactive and exhausted, or cause them to shut down their senses against the intensity of the stimuli" (p. 228).
- Birren (1978) discusses the impact of color. Red increases high energy and encourages creative thinking, while the color blue can be calming and help focus and concentration.
- To enhance concentration, use neutrals and subtle hues such as soft yellow, sandstone, soft peach, pale green, soft olive tones, beige, pale or light green, and blue-green (Olds, 2001).

Suggestions

- Paint walls with a fresh coat of off-white or neutral-tone paint. This provides the classroom with a calming backdrop.
- Select a contrasting neutral or cool color, and use it to paint bookshelves, dividers, and other pieces of furniture.
- To decrease environmental distractions, limit the number of colors in the classroom to two or three.
- Eliminate the need to cover bulletin boards by painting them the same neutral color as painted shelves and furniture. Be sure to receive permission from building administrators before painting over bulletin boards!
- Renew old furniture by giving it a refreshing coat of paint.
- Remove over-stimulating rugs, curtains, pillows, beanbags, and peripherals that contribute to color overload.
- Think neutral or subtle hues. Neutral backgrounds provide a backdrop for display of the ongoing work of the children as well as products of learning experiences.
- Reconsider the use of material with prints or patterns, as the intensity of pattern and variety of color may contribute to over-stimulation.
- Consider painting the walls a neutral color and allowing the children's projects to provide the classroom with color. Displaying children's work will add meaningful color to the environment and serve as a way to document the learning process.

"After" Photos

Painting shelves and bulletin boards with a cool color that contrasts to a classroom's wall color provides a background that helps highlight the objects and children's projects displayed on the shelves and bulletin boards. This also eliminates the need to cover bulletin boards with background paper and a border.

Neutral contrasting colors for shelving units and other furniture pieces help to define these elements as well as provide a fresh, aesthetically pleasing atmosphere.

"Before" Photo

First impressions tell a great deal about the educational philosophy of the teacher. A classroom's physical environment can either say, "This is a classroom for children," or, "This is the teacher's classroom." What first impression does your classroom make?

Welcoming and Inviting

According to Hart (1998), children must feel safe and secure in their environment in order to learn. A daily positive first impression or feeling of welcome and invitation to enter a classroom at the beginning of the day speaks to children and their families.

Key Points

- Reflect upon the experience of entering an unwelcoming space. How did that experience feel? Does such a space encourage learning or exploring new ideas? Feeling welcome and comfortable in an environment is foundational to learning.
- Emotions are a key factor in preparing a welcoming and inviting classroom and preparing the brain for learning. As Robert Sylwester says, "Emotions drive attention, create meaning, and have their own memory pathways" (as cited in Hart, 1998).

- Music can create a welcoming and inviting climate. In addition, several studies show that music can stimulate the parts of the brain responsible for memory recall (Sousa, 2001).
- Jensen (2001) recommends four to eight plants per 900 square feet of classroom. Plants not only clean the air, they also aesthetically enhance an environment.
- According to Marian Diamond (2006), providing an environment that fosters love, encouragement, warmth, and caring is a crucial component in determining academic success.
- Trawick-Smith (1992) states that classroom environments should be inviting, aesthetically pleasing, familiar, and friendly.
- A physical environment that incorporates some soft elements speaks to children, helping them feel safe and secure to explore (Greenman, 1988).

Suggestions

- Clean and organize classroom space. Create small work spaces for children to use individually and collaboratively. Design the space to enable children to move about comfortably and safely. An open environment invites children to move and explore according to their needs and learning styles.
- Use music throughout the day. Designate a space for musical equipment and supplies. Use different genres of music for different purposes. Play soothing, quiet music to welcome children to the classroom each day and ease the transition from home to school. Use upbeat music with a faster pace to set a tone for clean-up time.
- Post procedures for beginning the day with photographs that represent children implementing those procedures.
- Bring live plants into the classroom. Palms, rubber plants, spider plants, and peace lilies are safe and easy to care for.
- Add homelike elements, such as curtains, fabrics, pillows, area rugs, and plants. These bring softness and comfort to the environment.
- Remember to de-clutter. Organized space that is simple and not over-stimulating welcomes children. It helps them enter the classroom and prepare for the day of meaningful learning.

"After" Photos

Create a space that is open and well-organized with smaller spaces for focused work.

Take photographs of the children implementing beginning-of-the-day procedures and post those photos in the entrance area.

Welcome children each morning in the entrance area with a new message that requires a response.

"After" Photos

Place plants throughout the classroom to oxygenate the air and add to the aesthetics of the environment. Providing the children an accessible source of music, such as a portable CD player and CDs, encourages the use of music throughout the day.

Elements such as quilts on display, curtains, fabrics, photos, pets, and plants add softness and a homey comfort.

Pillows and rugs add softness and provide children with different seating choices. They also accommodate the learning styles of individual children and offer non-traditional seating positions for extended reading.

Sense of Community

Creating a sense of community in the classroom motivates children to become engaged in their work. When children and teachers work together to create procedures, plan events, actively engage, problem-solve, and reflect on living and learning in the classroom, true community can emerge. In learning communities, caring relationships are formed. These positive relationships impact children's academic success. Children feel safe in an environment free of threats. This provides a foundation that readies the body and mind for new knowledge, challenges, questions, practice, and reflection. It sets the stage for *meaningful learning* to occur.

"Before" Photo

In many classrooms there is not a designated place where a whole class can gather to greet one another, plan, review, discuss, and share. Or, the space provided for large group gatherings is cluttered, cramped, and lacks proper tools for documenting discussion, reflection, and planning.

Key Points

- According to Hart (1998), a child must feel safe and secure in an environment to be able to learn.
- Children in positive environments are likely to experience enhanced memory, learning, and feelings of self-esteem (Sylwester, 1995).
- Jensen (1998) suggests incorporating real-world problems into the classroom. Involving children in problem-solving provides opportunities for higher-level thinking.
- Problem-solving helps promote creative, meaningful judgment, according to Hileman (2006).
- According to Eisenberg & Mussen (1989), children are more likely to be cooperative and helpful toward one another if they are in a relaxed environment and engaged in interesting activities.
- Schedules appropriate for the children's age level and predictable routines provide consistency that helps to create a positive learning climate.

Suggestions

- Take photographs of the children, teachers and aides. Display these throughout the room or in a central location to welcome the children as they enter.
- Invite the children to bring in photographs of their families. Frame and display these around the room to let children and their families know they are an important part of the learning process.
- Create a designated large group gathering space in your room. Be sure it is free of clutter and has ample space for the children to sit comfortably and participate. Provide writing surfaces (whiteboards, interactive whiteboards, easels, flip charts, or individual whiteboards) as well as writing tools to capture thoughts and ideas of the large group.
- Add a shelf or designate nearby shelf space to display artifacts that relate to the current study or discussion topic.
- Involve children in the creation of daily schedules and procedures for the class. Involving children in this process makes the learning and learning climate more meaningful for them. Refer to Susan Kovalik and Karen Olsen's book (2005), *Exceeding Expectations: A User's Guide to Implementing Brain Research in the Classroom* for a step-by-step guide on how to develop procedures and create a positive sense of community.
- Jensen (1998) suggests providing choices relative to content, projects, resources, and processes for learning for children, making learning more relevant, personal, and engaging.
- One of the most important tasks educators have is to create a caring classroom environment that is brain-compatible and meaningful for *all* children.

"After" Photos

Designate a space for large group gathering. Begin the day greeting one another and planning for the day's events. Use the space throughout the day to gather and brainstorm ideas, problem-solve, discuss and share ideas, and present knowledge and skills.

Insert photos of children and teachers into frames to provide a warm welcome to those who enter the classroom. In addition to the welcome, the photographs show the community of learners in that classroom.

"After" Photos

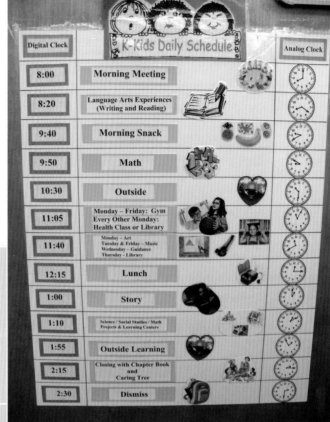

Make a schedule of the day visible at the children's level. Use pictures to depict events and people. The schedule will become more meaningful and purposeful when you involve children in its creation.

Using real photographs of spaces in the room is meaningful to the children. The charts will guide the children to specific areas and materials to use during different blocks of time throughout the day (for example: literacy block). Children can become more responsible for their learning tasks when they have opportunities to practice. In addition, they can work with or guide others, creating a sense of community in the process.

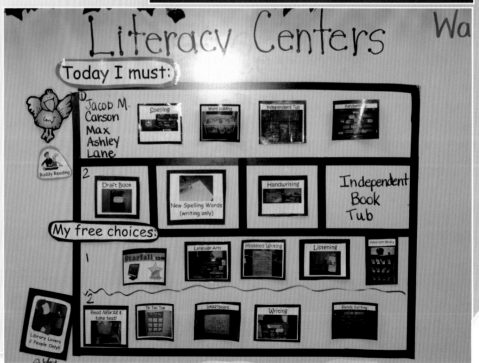

A Room to Learn

Capture children demonstrating life skills throughout the day.
Use the photographs to display these skills.

We are demonstrating skills for learning and life...

Communication

Responsibility

Cooperation

Perseverance

Friendship

Place reminders about skills for living throughout the building.
This potted plant is a daily reminder on a table in the common area.
Demonstrating these skills contributes to the creation of a community
of learners within the school. It also impacts the community at large
when children and their family members carry these skills into society.

Commentary

Teacher Comments

- Having a CD player and CDs available and organized in the meeting area allows me to use music for transitions throughout the day. For example, I use certain music selections to signal the beginnings and ends of different parts of the day. I also use music as a learning tool and to set the mood in the classroom.

- The childen will be bigger at the end of the year than they were at the beginning. Children need to have enough space to sit comfortably in the large group meeting space.
- Adding a visual component to the daily schedule has helped children self-regulate and feel a sense of community. The visual component incorporates literacy and math concepts with representations of the time and sequence of the day's events.
- Regularly scheduled times for sharing are important community-building events. Having a large group area gives the children the space they need to share with one another. Children anticipate their opportunity to share with others. They also learn to listen and respond with appropriate questions and comments.

Consultant Comment

- Previously I found that in many classrooms the procedures and class schedules were not in place or were not created with all members of the classroom community, nor were they posted for children to use as a reference. I found that when returning to classrooms after conducting professional development, one of the first steps teachers would take to improve their classroom environments was to create and display classroom procedures and daily schedules. The teachers discovered that children were more engaged and focused in their learning as a result of constructing the procedures, routines, and schedules together.

Principal Comment

- The school environment and the culture it reflects is not fluff. It lays the foundation for child and parent involvement.

The Classroom Arranged for Learning and Positive Learning Interactions

Use the *Primary Educator's Environment Checklist* (see page 181) to assess classroom learning environments and to examine the following topics: **Room Arrangement**, including spaces for small group work and collaboration, defined meeting areas for large group work and individual workspaces; and **Seating Choices**. Seating choices are important for social learning because they allow children the flexibility to work in physical and emotional comfort. These elements contribute to the successful design of *social learning* environments that promote learning as well as positive learning interactions.

Room Arrangement

Workspace arrangement is one of the first organizational elements to consider when designing a classroom to engage all children.

"Before" Photos

Many classrooms lack some or all of the key workspaces: individual workspace, small group workspace, large group workspace, and large group meeting space.

Key Points

- When arranging the room, create four spaces in the classroom environment: individual workspace, small group workspace, large group workspace, and a large group meeting space.

- Create spaces to meet the children's various needs. Address various learning styles (Dunn, Dunn, & Perrin, 1994) and multiple intelligences (Gardner, 1983) by providing spaces where children may work individually, in small groups, and large groups.
- Being flexible with room arrangement encourages the teacher to incorporate movement and active learning experiences throughout the day, allowing children the opportunity to move frequently as they learn. According to neurophysiologist Carla Hannaford (2005), "the neural connections between the motor cortex and the formal reasoning area of the frontal lobe underscore the importance of movement to thought processing" (p. 101).

Suggestions

- Offer space options that allow varying teaching strategies and learning opportunities to better meet the needs of the individuals and the group.
- Arrange learning spaces in a flexible way that can create opportunities for movement instead of having the children sit still at individual desks. Varying the space encourages active participation in the learning process, instead of passive reception of information with the children sitting in one static position throughout the day.
- Provide spaces for individual work. Include chairs, beanbags, individual seating cubes, pillows, and computer workstations.
- Create spaces for small group work. Add tables of various shapes and sizes with portable white boards and flip charts to create spaces for small group instruction.
- Think about a large group workspace to use for short periods of direct instruction or sharing with the whole group. Mount an interactive white board at the front of a gathering space. Consider a cluster of tables or small groups of tables dispersed throughout the room in specifically designated areas or centers. Ensure there is adequate seating for all the children.
- Remember, a large group meeting area is space that says "we are a community of learners." Create and value this space as it encourages cooperation and sharing of ideas. When children have opportunities to share, listen, respond, and problem-solve with one another, they are learning skills that will transfer to everyday life. The children develop respectful real world listening and communication skills.

"After" Photos

To meet the needs of children's various learning styles, provide options for individual workspace. An informal design such as this carpeted area with pillows and beanbags offers children an opportunity to work in a small group or alone in a relaxed setting. A formal design such as this uncluttered tabletop workspace provides a non-distracting place for a child to work alone in a more structured setting.

Clipboards provide a portable, hard-surfaced individual work area. Attach a pencil or pen for immediate use.

A small table, easel, and nearby shelving provide a small group workspace that allows for direct instruction, small group reading, and discussions.

"After" Photos

Small group work can take place in defined center areas to reduce distraction.

Desks clustered together create space for small group work and can also be useful when seating the whole class together at one time.

Tables allow for small group work. By having one seat per child it is possible to use the same space for large group work when necessary. Consider arranging the tables in the middle of the room (as pictured here) or throughout the room in center or workspaces.

Gathering in a large group for morning meetings, planning, reflecting, and celebrating learning can all take place in a single area specifically designed for this purpose. Adding a carpet and a variety of seating options also enables this space to function as a comfortable reading area later in the day.

In many classrooms children sit in the same position for extended periods of time. Requiring children to remain in formal seated positions without freedom to move may be inadvertently reducing the children's motivation throughout the day.

Seating Choices

Decisions about how to arrange seating in a classroom have a real impact on children's learning. Be considerate of children's individual learning styles by offering a variety of engaging choices in seating.

Key Points

- Provide a variety of seating choices, including options that are soft, hard, moveable, or stable. Dispersing seating designed for individuals, pairs, or small groups throughout the room will better meet the learning needs and styles of individual children.

Suggestions

- In addition to traditional seating, offer choices such as pillows, beanbags, couches, futons, floor seats, stools, benches, and therapy or exercise balls.
- Offer seating options that allow the teacher to vary teaching strategies and provide learning opportunities for individual children as well as small and large groups.
- Match seating to the activity. For activities requiring collaboration, use group seating options like couches, small tables, and benches.
- Have a variety of moveable and flexible seating options available throughout the room.
- Provide some seating options that allow for movement. Examples include rocking chairs, therapy or exercise balls, chairs on wheels, and chairs with adjustable seats.
- Remember that standing is also an option. According to the research of Max Vercruyssen, PhD., of the University of Southern California, as cited in Jensen (2000), "When subjects were asked to stand, their heart rate increased by 10 beats per minute on average. Standing up...creates more attentional arousal, speeds up information processing by 5%–20%, and increases blood flow and oxygen to the brain by 10%–15%"(p.170).
- Consider including a standing work table set to the appropriate height for the children.

"After" Photos

Inexpensive benches with attached pillows create a seating choice for an individual or pair of children.

Lofts provide children with comfortable, relaxed seating options.

Rugs, pillows, and cushions provide comfortable options that are easy to clean or replace when worn.

Provide seating options for children who are bodily/kinesthetic learners, such as rocking chairs and floor seats that wobble and allow children to rock.

Commentary

Teacher Comments

- Before, I think my room arrangement made it hard for children to work in groups. Since I started using tables, I've found that my children work together naturally.
- Working with children in small groups allows me to personalize instruction more to meet the individual needs of the learners.
- Clearly defined work areas to be used for different types of learning activities assist learners in becoming more responsible for their own learning. As the teacher, being able to offer the individual learner the opportunity to work independently or in a small group means I am creating learning situations that are more meaningful for the learner, thus more likely to engage the child in the learning process.
- The environment I have now supports social learning. It makes transitions easier. Children are demonstrating better citizenship all day because they are responsible for their own behavior.
- Working to improve the environment infused new life into our school. It was kind of like getting a house remodeled. All of a sudden we were looking at our classrooms differently, stepping back and saying, "Is this what I want my children to live in for 6 ½ hours a day?"

Consultant Comment

- Teachers worked hard to rid their classrooms of excess storage, furniture, file cabinets, and other items in an effort to allow for a room arrangement that includes a variety of spaces for individual, small group, and large group work. This led to thinking about providing instruction and learning opportunities that were more non-traditional and constructivist.

Principal Comment

- Using classroom environments as a focus for professional development has had a far greater impact on our school than I had imagined. My initial goal was to use this topic as a way to help teachers create a "friendlier environment." After initiating professional development, we found that developing our environments was supporting our teaching in unexpected ways. We were able to move from a traditional design to a more constructivist design. Social learning and purposeful learning became hallmarks of our instruction. Children became active participants in the learning process as the teachers became more adept at designing their environments.

A Room to Learn

The Organized Classroom Physically Arranged for Focused Learning

Use the *Primary Educator's Environment Checklist* (page 181) to assess classroom learning environments and examine the following topics: **Learning Centers and Stations, Personal Space for Children,** and **Teacher Space.** These elements contribute to the successful design of an organized classroom that is physically arranged for focused learning to occur in a *purposeful learning* environment.

Learning Centers and Stations

Learning centers or workstations provide children an opportunity to practice skills and play with newly learned concepts. An organized classroom will teach children the life skill of responsibility as they choose materials and "play with learning." In addition, learning centers and stations provide children opportunities to work alone or with others while constructing new knowledge and skills.

"Before" Photo

In some primary classrooms the only learning centers or stations focus on technology, with the centers arranged along walls in a linear fashion, so that children work individually.

Key Points

- Jensen (1998) suggests providing choices in the learning environment in an effort to increase motivation and maintain attention. Providing learning centers or stations where children may work makes learning more relevant and personal.
- Children need to practice or "play" with learning. They learn by doing. Active exploration and playing with concepts—alone and with others—makes learning purposeful.
- Rushton, Eitelgeorge, & Zickafoose (2003), connect Australian educator Brian Cambourne's Conditions of Learning, a theory of learning as it applies to literacy, to the classroom environment. They suggest that learning environments provide opportunities for children to play with learning and explore concepts. Centers offer choice in the classroom environment, which in turn addresses the individual differences and needs of all children.
- The use of learning centers allows for differentiation of instruction in general education, special education, and inclusive classrooms. They provide opportunities for children to learn in a variety of ways. The use of learning centers allows for small group instruction to occur while other children practice and review skills in other centers. Children engage in *purposeful learning* by practicing what they learn (King-Sears, 2007).

Suggestions

- Establish clearly defined areas for learning. Begin by adding the following centers: literacy (reading/library), writing, math, science, social studies, and technology.
- Arrange technology so that it allows for individual, partner, and small group use.
- Teach thematically, focusing on science and social studies standards for theme topics. In the literacy and math centers, reinforce standards by enhancing centers according to themes or topics that connect over multiple content areas.
- Add literacy centers or workstations to reinforce and teach concepts, develop skills, and offer opportunities for children to play with learning. Working alone and with others, children will strengthen newly gained knowledge and skills.
- Use shelving, furniture, and plants to divide learning centers. Be sure all areas of the room are visible at all times from the adult's view.
- In addition to tables, create learning centers and workstations with area rugs, risers, home-like furniture, and benches.
- Create learning center spaces that speak to children. Decorating these spaces with photographs, real artifacts, as well as documentation of the children's learning and their use of the materials in the learning center will invite children to the space and make content areas visible to adults. This encourages reflection for the children and adults in the classroom, as well as serving to represent children's learning processes for adults (teachers as well as parents and guardians).
- Arrange centers and workstations throughout the room, locating quiet centers near one another (reading/library, literacy stations, technology). Separate the quiet centers from active learning centers for exploration (math/manipulatives, science, and social studies).
- Incorporate various materials to meet the children's multiple learning styles and levels of learning. Organize the materials for easy access, use, and return.
- Designing learning centers and stations in the primary classroom allows children to extend and enhance their learning. Add a variety of interesting materials and choices to the centers, encouraging the children to explore these centers through their preferred learning styles (Dunn, Dunn & Perrin, 1994) and intelligences (Gardner, 1983).
- Creating aesthetically pleasing spaces by adding plants, varied lighting, and soft items will draw children to learning centers.
- Create a small, soft space for quiet reflection or problem-solving.

"After" Photos

Arrange technology centers or stations for individual, partner, and small group work. Space these areas around the room for use throughout the day.

Use floor space, risers, benches, and tables for learning center or station work. Children can work individually, with a partner, or in a small group.

Keep the writing and listening centers close yet separate. In the above photo, the book display in between the two centers includes literature that can enhance the theme of study throughout the room. In the listening center the inclusion of hard-back seating, soft pillows, rug space, and a bench offer children choices in seating while they listen to or read a story.

"After" Photos

This literacy station uses wall space and a pocket chart to offer children the opportunity to play with learning at the level that is appropriate for them.

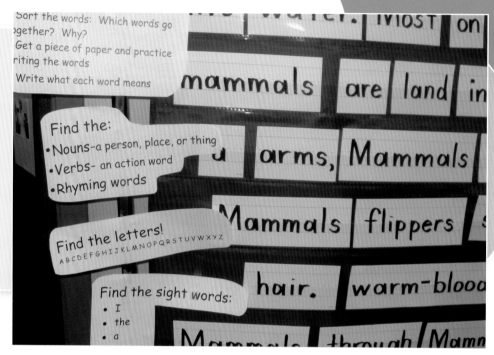

Sort the words: Which words go together? Why?
Get a piece of paper and practice writing the words
Write what each word means

Find the:
• Nouns–a person, place, or thing
• Verbs– an action word
• Rhyming words

Find the letters! ABCDEFGHIJKLMNOPQRSTUVWXYZ

Find the sight words:
• I
• the
• a

Clearly defining and labeling specific areas of a station or center helps to direct the children's learning experiences.

Clearly defined and labeled shelves allow children to access materials they can use for further exploration and to play with learning.

"After" Photos

Create a space where individual children can go to cool down, reflect, and problem-solve solutions to conflicts or other problems in the classroom. Jane Nelsen's (2000) *Positive Discipline in the Classroom* recommends a *Wheel of Choice* as a tool for problem-solving.

Soft pillows and rugs define this space and welcome children to the area. Including fun items (like the games in this photo) in the center gives children quick access to fun educational experiences as well as the space to work and play together.

In many classrooms the only space that children call their own is that of a locker outside the classroom or the desk that has been assigned to them.

Personal Space for Children

Providing space for children to store personal belongings (such as coats, hats, and backpacks) and artifacts that represent their learning (such as portfolios, draft writing books, and other representations from their learning experiences) sends the message that the classroom is a space that is shared by all. Providing the children personal space gives them the opportunity to develop skills such as organization, initiative, and responsibility.

Key Points

- Providing individual space for children to store belongings and artifacts that are representative of the children's learning sends a caring message. According to Maslow's (1987) *Hierarchy of Needs*, providing personal space for children contributes to the third tier in the hierarchy: belongingness and love. Children feel accepted and know that they are members of the learning community when they have space for personal belongings and they see artifacts that represent their learning.

"After" Photos

Portfolios labeled with names and photographs (blocked for confidentiality in this photo) help contribute to the sense of community. Children in this classroom know they belong and that their work is valued.

Suggestions

- Provide individual personal space by assigning a cubby or locker space for each child.
- Consider using binders or hanging folders to collect artifacts that are representative of each child's learning. Store these in places accessible to the children. Help the children develop their sense of responsibility by encouraging them to add to the collection.
- Consider asking the school's maintenance department or others with carpentry skills to build cubbies or lockers for the classroom.
- To decrease clutter and the feeling of overstimulation, consider covering open cubbies with a neutral-colored material.

Non-commercially purchased lockers (like those in the photo) allow third graders to have personal space. Doors hide the sometimes-messy contents. Children in this class personalize their space by labeling and decorating the inside doors of their lockers. In addition to creating personal space, the locker units (consisting of 4–5 individual lockers) are useful as a way to separate learning centers and work zones.

Providing a basket labeled "Personal Best" encourages the children to work hard in an effort to achieve their best. These are two examples of how personalized space and materials can emphasize the value of the children and their work.

"After" Photos

A shoe organizer serves as a container for individual headsets. Asking children to design a personal label for their individual pockets sends a message to the children that they are important members of the classroom community.

Covering cubbies with neutral-colored material creates an aesthetically pleasing effect, hiding contents within, while providing space for children's personal belongings. Securing this material with Velcro® makes periodic removal and cleaning easy.

In many classrooms, large teacher desks end up serving as catch-all spaces, and eventually become non-functional, simply occupying space.

Teacher Space

In traditionally designed classrooms the teacher's desk and space is in the front of the room. Consider reducing the amount of space teacher furniture and materials take up by creating a classroom design with workspace that is available to all learners, including the teacher.

Key Points

- According to Morrison (2000), organization is a key measure of good teaching and teacher effectiveness. Effective teachers create supportive learning environments to maximize children's engagement in their learning.
- Model organization for children by maintaining a clean, organized work space.
- Organizing teacher workspace and materials saves time and provides the opportunity to spend more time with individuals and small groups of children throughout the day.

Suggestions

- Take the time to clean the teacher desk and surrounding space on a regular schedule.
- Remove additional teacher desks, such as those used by teaching assistants.
- When the children are not in the classroom, take some time to organize and store materials in closets and other closed storage spaces.
- Organize the materials so they are easily accessible throughout the day.
- Reduce the amount of teacher space in the classroom. Do not allow teacher desk and storage areas to consume large areas of the learning space.
- Model organization for the children. Children learn this very important skill just by observing how their teachers organize, store, and access materials.
- Be flexible about teacher workspace. Rather than designating one computer for teacher-only work, work at one of the computers the children use throughout the day. During planning times and after school, use the children's tables to complete work.
- Consider removing the teacher desk from the classroom. Replace it with a smaller piece of furniture that can hold the necessary plans and materials for the day's lessons.

"After" Photos

Replace the teacher desk with a smaller desk or another piece of furniture that can hold necessary items for the day's lessons.

Children and teachers can share storage and workspace. Use bins to store materials and containers for shared supplies. This allows for easy transport, use, and storage.

Commentary

Teacher Comments

- The environment is safer for children because I am able to see them in their centers.
- When I gave up my teacher desk, I gave up the clutter.
- I learned that teacher space in the classroom can be minimal. All that is needed is a small space for materials and tools for the day.

Consultant Comment

- Organization—or lack thereof—is obvious to the classroom visitor and has a significant impact on children's learning. Often those who live in the environment daily are unaware of its lack of organization. Designating space for the children's and teacher's belongings and focusing on the organizational elements of this space incidentally teaches a very important skill. When we add or redesign space for the children's and teacher's belongings, and create learning centers and stations, teachers notice more purpose in the learning. Children are proud to be members of the learning community and demonstrate responsibility throughout the day.

Principal Comment

- A disorganized classroom is not a private matter. It is a public display and compromises the reputation of the teacher and the learning that takes place in the classroom.

Organized Materials in the Classroom to Promote Engagement in Learning

CHAPTER

7

Use the *Primary Educator's Environment Checklist* (see page 181) to assess classroom learning environments and examine the following topics: **Clutter, Materials Available for Learning,** and **Organized Materials.** These elements contribute to the successful design of an organized classroom whose physical arrangement and organization encourage *responsible learning*.

Clutter

It is critical to clean and de-clutter on a regular basis. Live by the phrase "less is more." Many children are distracted by the overabundance of "stuff" in the classroom. This includes storage, items hanging from the ceiling, as well as posters and commercially purchased materials that take up bulletin board and wall space.

"Before" Photos

In many primary classrooms, storage space is at a premium. It is important not to allow furniture, extra materials, and supplies to creep out and take up classroom space that can be used for learning purposes. Clean and reduce clutter to gain back learning space.

Key Points

- Think about places people go—to shop or work on projects—that require focus, action, and results. If these locations are unorganized and highly cluttered, can a person focus on the task at hand? Is it simple or difficult to find the materials needed to get the job done? Examine the classroom from this perspective. Is the classroom de-cluttered and clean? Are materials organized? Can the children find what they need without difficulty? If not, it may be time to consider de-cluttering the classroom environment.

Suggestions

- Clean, throw out, organize, label, and prepare an organized environment. This helps children focus on the current learning topics.
- Throw out the items, papers, and materials that have been in the "I might use this someday" pile. Likely these are unnecessary and easily replaceable.
- Remove things hanging from the ceiling. They are distracting to learners.
- Create systems of organization. Organize similar materials in similar containers to give a visual cue that the materials belong together. (For example: math materials in containers with blue lids, science in containers with green lids.)
- Break the habit of saving everything. Many teachers save recycled materials (paper towel tubes, empty containers, and so on). These materials take up valuable space. Save a few and stop. If necessary, ask families to donate these materials when the children are working on a project that requires them.
- Clean, clean, clean!
- Pitch, pitch, pitch it!

"After" Photos

Ridding areas of excess furniture and unused materials (see "before" photos on page 104) provides space for housing organized materials that children can access quickly and safely during the learning day.

Notice how the labels and the clear containers make the organization easy to see and the materials easy to find.

Materials Available for Learning

According to Hillman (1989), creating a positive learning climate—one where children feel safe when trying new ideas and taking risks—nurtures a love of learning and assists children in developing a strong sense of self. Designing classroom space to incorporate a variety of materials children use in the learning process is validating to those children. Providing a choice of materials and allowing adequate time for children to explore the materials enable children to build and demonstrate their understanding of concepts and skills.

"Before" Photo

Commercial materials consisting of textbooks and worksheets are the preferred mode of learning in this classroom.

Key Points

- Make sure the materials in the classroom are there for children's use. Reduce the number of teacher-purchased materials and increase the number of teacher- and child-created artifacts that represent the teaching and learning cycle taking place in the classroom.
- The concept of having materials available for learning extends beyond the classroom and the children assigned to the class. Families and other visitors can contribute to learning in the classroom.

Suggestions

- Organize materials in appropriately-sized containers for easy transport to work areas. Label them well. Store them on shelves accessible to children.
- Organize supplies (such as pencils, markers, and scissors) to place on tables for community use. This provides children with opportunities to learn to share and demonstrate responsibility.
- When possible, use real objects and objects the children have created, as opposed to pictures or commercially purchased replicas.
- Provide a variety of materials for the children to use.
- Encourage children to take risks and construct their own knowledge.
- Provide a variety of tools, such as digital cameras, tape recorders, and video cameras for collecting data.
- Provide clipboards, journals, and drawing materials the children can use to take notes and represent their learning.
- Provide materials such as playdough, clay, and recycled materials with which the children can make three-dimensional representations of their learning.
- Provide magazines, computers, and printers for gathering photographs of the topics the children are studying.

"After" Photos

Teacher-created materials (such as those shown here) guide the children as they arrive in the morning and choose materials to use as they begin the day.

Encourage children to "have-a-go" at tasks as they practice newly gained knowledge and skills.

Labeling containers clearly and storing them on low shelves enables children to demonstrate responsibility as they access, choose, use, and return materials.

"After" Photo

Keep supplies in containers that are easy to carry, clearly labeled, and easy to reach.

Organized Materials

Maria Montessori (1870–1952) was among the first theorists to stress the value of the visual appeal of learning materials and overall classroom aesthetics. This emphasis is visible today in classrooms around the world. Keeping materials clean and organized is part of the learning plan. Exposing children to the benefits of organization and encouraging the respectful use of materials provides children with skills necessary throughout life. Respect for the environment begins when the teacher prepares and organizes the learning space and materials for children to use as they explore concepts and develop skills (Montessori, 1949). *Responsible learning* is more apt to occur when materials are organized, well labeled, and accessible to the learners.

"Before" Photos

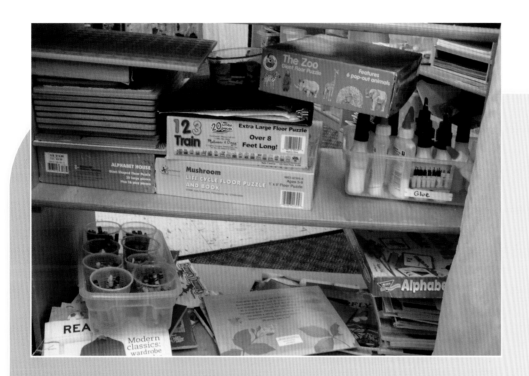

In many classrooms, materials are unorganized, difficult to locate, and displayed in visually unappealing ways.

Key Points

- Young children learn by doing, being involved in active exploration, and playing with concepts. Organized and accessible materials encourage *responsible learning*. Challenge children to think, ask questions, explore, and play with learning. This will help the children better understand and process their learning experiences.

Suggestions

- Clean, throw out, organize, and label materials.
- Label containers clearly. Use pictures and words in classrooms where children are still learning to read and write. Use words to label items in classrooms with older children who are reading.
- When using pictures to label containers of materials, photograph the actual material to ensure a perfect match when children are cleaning up.
- Arrange materials so the arrangement itself says, "Use me, be productive, process the learning."
- Use child-sized and moveable containers so the children can move and use the materials anywhere in the classroom or outdoors. Smaller containers, small buckets with handles, larger containers with wheels, and clear bins that the children can transport are appropriate.
- Store containers of materials on shelves where children can access and return them safely.
- Introduce materials to the children prior to placing the materials in centers or stations. Modeling care, storage, and proper use of materials to the children is necessary to maintain organization and teach responsibility.
- Organize teacher resources and materials as well as those for children. Teachers who can find what they need quickly are more prepared to meet individual needs. In addition, having a storage system in place that gives teachers access to supportive learning materials provides more time to take advantage of the "teachable moment" as new questions and ideas arise among the children. In the emergent curriculum approach it is necessary to have the children's and teacher's materials and resources thoughtfully organized for quick and easy access by all.

"After" Photo

Displaying the covers of books makes them more attractive to children and stimulates children's interest in the topics.

"After" Photos

Using clear containers, pictures, and words to label materials enables children to be independent when accessing materials as well as when putting them back after use. On the labels, consider including the names of the objects in a second language. This is a great way to enhance the children's learning.

Organize a variety of writing tools for easy access and transport. When children have access to materials they need, they spend less time hunting for tools and more time engaged in learning.

If you wish to limit children's access to stored materials, hang quilts (possibly quilts the children helped make) to cover shelves, as in this picture that shows books stored according to theme or topic. Or, use blinds to cover shelves and materials not being used. Be careful to shorten cords and keep them out of children's reach.

"After" Photos

Use large, clear storage containers for prop boxes (label these according to themes). Label containers by inserting a large index card inside the front of the container instead of labeling the outside of the container with markers or adhesive labels. Using clear containers helps teachers locate materials quickly, such as the materials stored above the cabinets in this photo.

Label each cabinet door and drawer to assist in locating items quickly and in returning materials to their proper place. This also makes it easier for teaching assistants, families, and volunteers to assist in the classroom.

Commentary

Teacher Comments

- I learned new vocabulary and a new skill: "Pitch it."
- We had always learned to save everything. I used to say, "Sure, I'll take it." Now I am much more discriminating.
- Do a redesign with a partner—this gives you someone to encourage you to "pitch it" and to cheer you on.
- This kind of organization makes finding materials a snap. Materials are all in clearly marked containers. I used to spend a large amount of time just searching for items. Now I can spend that time planning and working with children instead.
- It is like having another teacher in the room. Everything is readily available and the learning is uninterrupted.
- The environment is an additional teacher!

Consultant Comment

- When you live in a classroom day after day you don't see the distractions, clutter, or overstimulation created by excess materials, furniture, and storage that takes up space. As teachers, we think we might need that item some day, so we tend to keep everything. Have someone else work with you when de-cluttering your environment. This critical friend can help you let go of and organize materials in new ways that can help reduce overstimulation and make materials quickly available for learning.

Principal Comment

- Organization is a crucial and consistent element used when evaluating teachers and the effectiveness of teaching. Classrooms where teachers have spent time organizing the rooms and materials typically have more children engaged in learning. Engagement is a key factor in any successful learning process. Spending time on the organization of materials is well worth it!

A Room to Learn

Classroom Peripherals Representing the Learning Process and Learning Projects

Use the *Primary Educator's Environment Checklist* (see page 181) to assess classroom learning environments and examine the following topics: **Commercial Peripherals**, **Documentation of Learning**, and **Peripherals Representative of Learning**. Classroom peripherals are an important resource for teaching and learning. They are evidence of the learning process and they document the learning activities of accessing prior knowledge, planning, investigation, and elaboration. Peripherals are not classroom decorations. They are tools in the classroom environment that support *continuous learning*.

Commercial Peripherals

Peripherals are an underutilized tool for supporting children's achievement. Too often teachers use available wall space and bulletin boards only as areas for posting decorations for their room. These displays are frequently loosely connected to the teaching-learning process or disconnected from it altogether. For example, quarterly seasonal displays dominate many primary classrooms, but learning objectives for children are often only distantly related to the seasons.

Commercially purchased peripherals are a staple in the educational environment and they range in design from cute cutouts to posters that list rules for learning. It is useful to ask the following question when considering posting any peripheral: In what ways does this object represent or enhance the children's engagement in the learning process? Commercial peripherals often do not capture or extend the learning, nor do they engage the children. Their information can be limited or difficult for children to understand, and they are often visually over-stimulating. Peripherals created with children during the learning process are more meaningful.

"Before" Photos

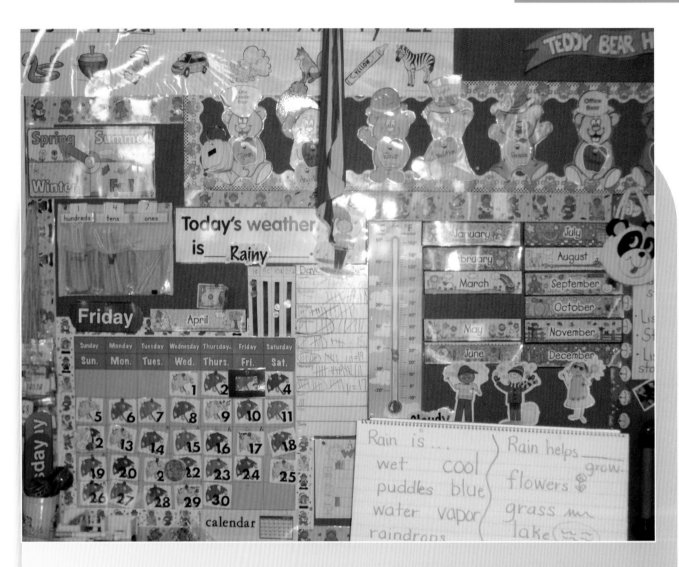

These peripherals are overpowering.
The purpose for each peripheral is lost
in the volume of visual stimulation.

Peripherals should support children's learning. The placement of these posters, near the ceiling in a classroom, limits their usefulness.

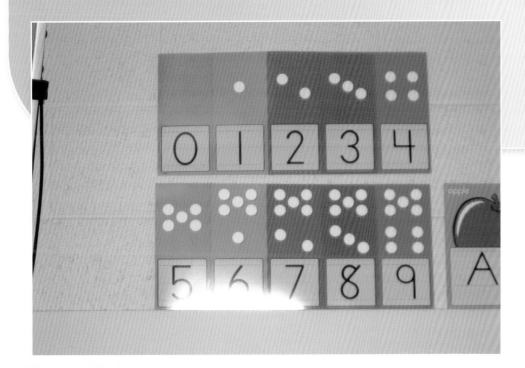

Key Points

- Thoughtful practitioners will use peripherals to engage children by celebrating the processes and products associated with learning. These visuals help children organize their learning (Katz, 1998).
- The brain synthesizes visual information both on a conscious and a subconscious level (Jensen, 2008). The messages children receive from the visuals in a classroom impact those children on both the academic and emotional level.
- Effective peripherals not only support children in their learning but also celebrate the learning process (Tarr, 2004).
- Early learners rely on physical representations as they develop their vocabulary and schema of abstract concepts (Piaget, 1963). Authentic artifacts make indispensable peripherals in the primary classroom.
- Think about the classroom as a piece of real estate. It is a dwelling for 15–25 individuals for a minimum of 6 ½ hours, five days each week. All of those individuals have a stake in the property. Commercial peripherals are products created outside of the classroom experience. In essence, they add "outside parties" to the already crowded environment.

Suggestions

- Create charts as a classroom group to establish procedures and to capture the learning. Post these as references for the children to use during ongoing conversations about the topics of study and for the children to use during their small group and independent learning time.
- Avoid the trap of "decorating" the room (Tarr, 2004). Some teachers may want to begin the school year with bare walls, and then send a letter to children's families explaining that the room is intended to support the children's learning and that the walls over time will begin to fill with images that reflect their children's learning.
- Don't allow "must have" commercial peripherals to be space hogs. Minimize the amount of real estate they consume.
- Display authentic peripherals. Objects and photographs that provide foundational ideas for the topics of study should be prominent in the classroom.

- Artifacts of the children's work serve as motivating reminders of the learning.
- Peripheral placement is important, not only aesthetically but also academically. Children must be able to access the information peripherals present (Matteson, D., personal communication, January 14, 2010). Peripherals that hang from the ceiling are hard for children to see, and thus rarely support continuous learning. Likewise, the surfaces above whiteboards are not locations for peripherals in classrooms of young children. While this is the most common place to put up commercial number lines and alphabet charts, children often have difficulty accessing information in such locations. Children tend instead to refer to charts that are on their desks or in their journals.
- Using too many peripherals is overwhelming to the learning environment. It becomes difficult to determine the purpose and function of the individual postings in a crowded display. Look for ways to reduce the amount of space peripherals occupy in the classroom.

This teacher- and student-made math visual, if placed at an accessible height to the learner, becomes a learning tool for children to use when practiciting skill development.

"Before" and "After":
Focused Peripherals

In the first picture, book jackets and character cutouts decorate a bulletin board that takes up one entire wall of the classroom. The second picture shows a more focused bulletin board that allows some wall space to be used for other purposes.

"After" Photo

This display highlights a variety of authentic, interesting resources. In addition, these peripherals support a sense of community and encourage reflection.

"Before" Photo

Consider the effectiveness of this presentation of peripherals. Here, children's work from an instructional activity is displayed alongside commercial peripherals that have a different focus.

Documentation of Learning

Documentation in the form of classroom peripherals serves as a foundational tool for a classroom of continuous learning. The use of peripherals should either help capture the current learning or extend the learning process. Photos that represent the learning process are a type of peripheral that engages the learner.

"Before" Photo

Posting children's work is not the same thing as documenting their learning. The reflective teacher should ask: "How does this peripheral support children's learning and help them make connections to future learning?"

Key Points

- Children's engagement increases their learning. Teachers can use peripherals to help children connect with the learning process. Change these artifacts frequently in order to represent current areas of study. Effective peripherals not only support children in their learning but also celebrate the learning process (Tarr, 2004; Katz & Chard, 1996).
- Although assessment plays multiple roles in a classroom, the primary goal of assessment is to provide a more appropriate and meaningful education for the children. An NAEYC position paper from 2003 reflects this attitude. There, NAEYC indicates that the educator's objective is to, "Develop a systematic plan for assessment over time using authentic measures (those that assess children's real-world activities and challenges) and focusing on outcomes that have been identified as important. The primary goal in every case is to make the program (curriculum and teaching practices) as effective as possible so that every child benefits" (p. 12). It is a reciprocal process that informs the

teaching and learning cycle. For that reason, teachers can use a variety of tools for assessment, including quantitative data, work samples, video, projects, and portfolios. All of these artifacts can serve as peripherals that document children's learning.

● Use peripherals to represent and document parts of the learning process that are cohesive (thematic in approach) and represent higher-order thinking skills (Kovalik, 1993).

Suggestions

● Often learning does not result in a static product. Children at work in the block center, for example, might create an elaborate system of roadways and bridges. Create a documentation panel to capture such projects. This documentation can be as simple as taking a photo of the children at work and attaching quotes from the children about their work.

● Less really is more. Neat presentation is important. Be sure to attach all visuals securely to the walls. Remember the subtle, emotional messages that presentation creates. While neatness is a factor, having a professional-looking, commercially designed product is not.

● Use children's work to illustrate teaching points. Keep in mind, however, that isolated activities that are worksheet based, rote, or mundane, do not translate into useful peripherals.

● Posting children's work is not synonymous with documenting the learning. Plan learning experiences that require children to integrate a variety of skills. These experiences grow out of the foundational principles associated with a child-centered, constructivist philosophy. In such a classroom, children invariably create intriguing results. Results from learning activities that do not require synthesis of information or do not require children to think at higher levels will not serve as peripherals that stimulate further learning.

"After" Photos

This class has developed procedures for exploring mathematical ideas. A peripheral has been created to capture their process.

The teacher includes a photo of a child on this visual that the class has created to depict the stages of the writing process.

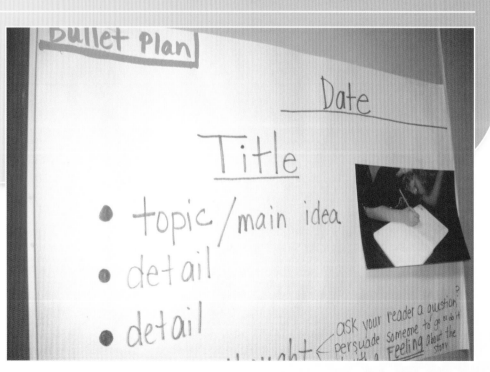

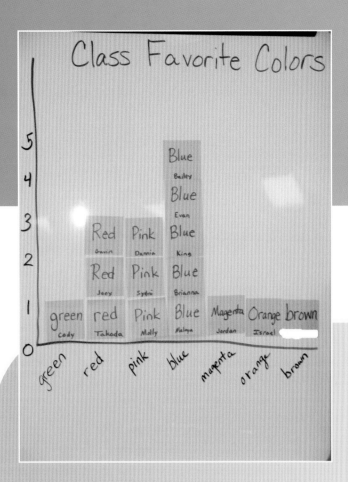

Class Favorite Colors

				Blue Bailey			
5				Blue Evan			
4							
3		Red Gavin	Pink Dannia	Blue King			
2		Red Joey	Pink Sydni	Blue Brianna			
1	green Cody	red Takoda	Pink Molly	Blue Malaya	Magenta Jordan	Orange Israel	brown
0							

green   red   pink   blue   magenta   orange   brown

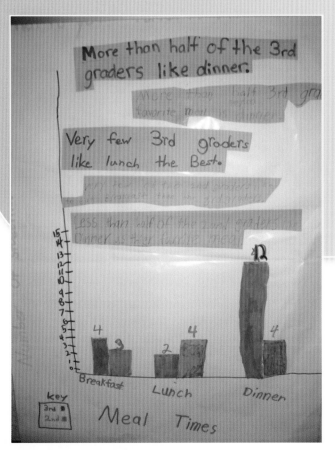

More than half of the 3rd graders like dinner.

Very few 3rd graders like lunch the Best.

More than half of the 3rd graders like dinner as their favorite meal.

15 14 13 12 11 10 9 8 7 6 5 4 3 2 1 0

4   3   2   4   12   4

Breakfast   Lunch   Dinner

key
3rd ■
2nd ▦

Meal Times

Children's projects serve as documentation of learning. Here are two examples of graphs used as peripherals. Notice the simplicity of these peripherals. The value of the kindergarten bar graph increases because it includes each child's name. The third grade bar graph captures children's learning through their reflective, summarizing statements.

Peripherals Representative of Learning

In a constructivist environment, children work together as a community of learners. The collaborative processes associated with this type of learning rely upon the foundation established through the social learning environment (see Chapter 5). Peripherals associated with the social learning environment are representative of collaborative learning and of learning that incorporates skills for positive living. Displays should demonstrate the value of children and their learning. Authentic work—work created by the children individually or in groups—must be at center stage. This indicates, to children and their families, the value of the work of the children in the classroom.

When assessing classrooms using the *Primary Educator's Environment Checklist* (see page 181), we often observe peripherals that are not representative of learning. The most common peripheral in this category is the commercial poster highlighting aspects of good citizenship. Also common are word walls that lack useful design and organization, resulting in a confusing connection with the children's learning processes.

"Before" Photo

This word wall attempts to use peripherals as an extension of the learning. As often happens, it is difficult for children to access the words visually because of their jumbled arrangement.

Key Points

● One strategy for helping children solidify their learning is to help them develop connections between what they know and new content (Marzano, 2003). Peripherals can serve as documentation of prior knowledge and provide an avenue for helping children see the links between different parts of the curriculum.

● Interactive peripherals help children make connections to the curriculum by increasing their engagement with the concepts being explored.

Suggestions

- Create interactive bulletin boards. Class projects that engage children with the real world are especially effective for creating these peripherals.
- Documentation panels representing collaborative work through pictures and narratives about the learning are beneficial by: 1) creating a sense of being a community of learners, and 2) helping children connect visually and emotionally with their learning (Project Zero & Reggio Children, Italy, 2001). Documentation can be as simple as taking and posting a photo of children working on a project.
- Take digital pictures of children working. While these photos can serve a variety of purposes, they are especially helpful in getting children to talk about their learning. This helps children develop their oral language skills, their sense of sequencing, and expands their engagement in the learning. Posting these pictures with quotations from the children (young children may dictate these quotations, while older children may write them) is an effective way of representing the learning. This is a great type of peripheral to display outside the classroom to help the families understand their children's learning processes.
- Create a digital documentation panel. Transfer pictures to a PowerPoint slide presentation. Play the slideshow using a classroom computer.
- In addition to traditional methods of assessment, use portfolios. When children select their own materials to include in the portfolio, they are more reflective. Note that worksheet-type assignments do not encourage children to reflect on their learning and their portfolio development.

This teacher has personalized the children's learning. They are identifying the vowels in their names.

The children in this third-grade classroom are creating a word wall; they are making visual representations of the words and using them in sentences.

"After" Photos

Setting up an actual thermometer outside the classroom provides a great peripheral the children can use as a source for data collection throughout the year.

Note that the teacher and children created the classroom procedures together. Displaying the children's signatures reminds them that they were included in the process of creating procedures.

Second Grade Rules
Created 7/16/09 by the Second Grade Class

1. Stay in control

2. Learn fair

3. Be nice

4. Respect our classroom

"Before" and "After":
Interactive Peripherals

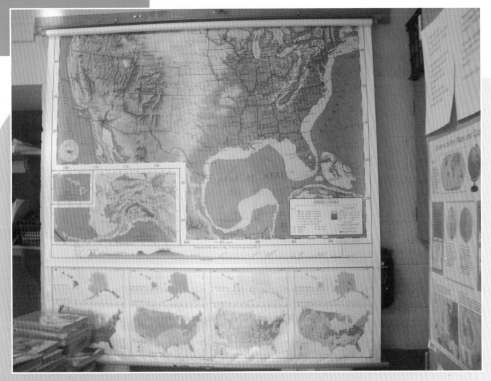

Compare the impact of these two map displays. Both groups of children are studying the United States. The second photo shows an interactive map the children created as part of a "Flat Stanley" project (Hubert, 1995). This book character, Flat Stanley, travels around the country with families and friends of the children in this class. As children pinpoint areas visited they learn about geography and mapping skills. This map demonstrates how a peripheral can serve as a resource and extension of the learning.

"After" Photos

This display shows children exploring science concepts and extending their learning through writing about the experience.

This child has selected pieces of work for a portfolio. He is including a reflective piece that invites his family members to notice particular features of the portfolio.

👓 Things to Notice . . .
While you look at my portfolio

Dear Family,
While you look at my portfolio with me I want you to notice these things about it.

1. I Wut you to see my blud f

2. I wut you to see my cims pihis

3. I wut you to see my pihro wah mach sue has with boys

These are things I think I do well.

1. I hac I am goo at mah

2. I hac I am gop at my jas boc

3. I hac Tot I am gop at my spelen

Please write a comment or a letter to me on the back of this sheet after we have looked at my portfolio.

Love,

Logan

This teacher has created a display that includes samples of the children's scientific writing.

"After" Photo

The teacher and children created common understandings about their goals for learning.

Commentary

Teacher Comments

- I decided it was not my classroom; it belonged to the children. I wanted to do something that would show the children that they were the learners and that their learning was of great value. I decided I would only use peripherals created either by us as a class, or by the children. The first time I began the school year with bare walls, I was terrified that the children's families and other teachers would think that I was "a bad teacher" because I didn't have my room decorated for the first day of school. It was a real paradigm shift. Of course, within days the walls were filled with evidence of learning.

- Documentation panels made a huge difference in the way I used peripherals. By the end of the year, my third graders were able to take pictures of themselves working on group projects. They inserted these photos into documentation panels they made using the computer. This became one strategy for them to articulate their learning in a meaningful way.

Consultant Comment

- Recall the phrase, "If the walls could talk," and consider the walls as a learning tool. They speak to children and adults. Walls can help reflect and refuel the learning process. Instead of "If the walls *could* talk," think "Wow! These walls *really* communicate about the learning taking place in this classroom."

Principal Comment

- It is crucial not to underestimate the role of peripherals in supporting and reflecting a dynamic child-centered classroom. When I first began a focus on creating child-centered classroom environments, I misjudged the importance of peripherals and saw them as "fluff." However, as I learned more about the principles of teaching and learning associated with high-quality primary classrooms, I recognized that peripherals are intricately associated with the learning climate and have great value in supporting children's educational achievement. I eventually saw that the peripherals in a classroom gave me insight into the teachers' application of principles associated with a constructivist philosophy. They are the representation of the learning to the main stakeholders in the classroom: the children.

The Classroom Ready for In-depth Study

The classroom ready for in-depth study is a classroom that uses inquiry and exploration as its guiding educational principles. Inquiry-based learning is the pedagogical target for the teacher who embraces a constructivist philosophy. The various components of the environment discussed in chapters three through eight provide teachers with ideas about how to design classrooms that promote children's active involvement in the learning process. These components also give teachers the freedom to structure inquiry-based learning for children in an organized and meaningful way. These environmental supports help children develop the skills they need to become involved, independent learners. Working in classrooms that lack these environmental supports makes it more difficult for children to develop the learning processes necessary to acquire new understanding and awareness about their worlds. In the primary classroom, the focus should be not only on content; educators must also teach children how to learn. Inquiry-based learning accomplishes both of these objectives. While there is some debate in academic circles about the precise meaning of the phrase "inquiry-based learning," in the context of this chapter it means learning that is child-centered, with a focus on both discovery *and* application of learning.

Inquiry-based learning relies on pedagogy that emphasizes in-depth study and creative problem-solving. Teachers in the inquiry-based classroom recognize that the process by which a child gains new understanding is rarely linear. A child gathers bits of information related to a point of inquiry. The child then acquires knowledge by exploring authentic sources, collecting data, and collaborating with other children and adults. As children share ideas and use the knowledge gained through exploration and study, they come to own their learning experiences. In this scenario, "the learner is mindfully managing input" (Fogarty, 1999, p. 78) and making applications that are personally meaningful. This description of children engaging in the learning process speaks to the importance of carefully structuring the learning environment.

The effective teacher must create learning opportunities that allow children to interact, experiment, investigate, and reflect upon their experiences. The teacher facilitates children's engagement by asking questions (Welch, Klopfer, Aikenhead, & Robinson, 1981). The types of questions the teacher asks are key to engaging children in the learning process. These are not questions with simple answers. They are open-ended questions that require reflective responses: "What were your thoughts when you did that? How does this remind you of _____ (another problem)? How does this change your thinking? How will you use this information?" Children, in turn, learn to ask questions of their own that support them in developing continuing hypotheses and explorations.

This structure for learning is founded on the principles for teaching and learning espoused by educational gurus like Dewey (1938/1997), Piaget (1963), Bruner (1966, 1983), and Vygotsky (1978) as well as by leading researchers and educators such as Diamond and Hopson (1998), Jensen (2001), Kovalik and Olsen (2005), Wolfe (2001), Gardner (1983), and Bredekamp and Rosegrant (1992). The classroom ready for in-depth study synthesizes the components of the other aspects of the learning environment to create a classroom in which children can engage in active learning. The processes and the products of such a classroom will reflect inquiry-based learning.

There is an observable, reciprocal interaction between the teacher, children, and the physical environment that culminates in child-centered, inquiry-based instruction. This chapter focuses on the evidence associated with this interactive process. The final aspect of the learning environment assessed through the *Primary Educator's Environment Checklist* (see page 181) is The Inquiry-based Learning Environment. The characteristics under review break into three separate areas: Planning and Collaboration, Research Resources, and Evidence of Inquiry-based Learning. Use the *Primary Educator's Environment Checklist* (see page 181) as a tool to quantify the evidence of inquiry-based learning.

Planning and Collaboration

Planning and Collaboration is one aspect of the **Classroom Ready for In-depth Study**. The *Primary Educator's Environment Checklist* (see page 181) outlines four observable features associated with collaborative learning: *Conversations, Planning, Graphic Organizers,* and *Sharing of Ideas and Findings*. Each of these features leads to a cohesive teaching and learning environment.

Conversations

Conversations are an integral part of active learning processes. Children become engaged in their learning as they respond to questions, exchange ideas, and design their work. Questioning plays a key role in the process. It encourages interaction ("What were you thinking about when you were looking at this?") and helps children remain focused on their goals ("How will you find the information that you need to include here?").

Teachers must remember that telling children how to do it "right" does not solidify their learning nor engage them in the process. Communication is a critical aspect of learning and is foundational both for planning the work and for articulating children's understanding. Dialogue impacts children's cognitive ability and creates the foundation for cooperative problem-solving and internalization of learning (Vygotsky, 1978).

Planning

Planning for learning is an important part of organizing the educational process. In the inquiry-based classroom, the teacher and the children engage in planning together. Teachers promote children's investment in an activity and help children internalize the activity's outcomes by providing interesting collaborative projects. These projects give the children a shared goal as well as the task of meeting that goal together. These projects provide children with the opportunity to discuss and challenge one another throughout the process. As they discover and discuss one another's ideas and perspectives on a project, the children experience cognitive dissonance. Through language, the children interact with and consider one another's differing perspectives. In doing so the children modify their own perceptions of the task at hand, and they grow by incorporating other children's ideas into their thinking (Vygotsky, 1978).

Graphic Organizers

Graphic organizers are one tool children can use to capture ideas they develop through discourse as well as to structure their learning. Conversations lead the children to define and organize their work. Graphic organizers are visual representations of that work that combine linguistic (words and phrases) and nonlinguistic elements (symbols that represent relationships) (Marzano, Pickering, & Pollock, 2001). However, because each type of organizer is designed for a specific purpose, children must know how to use graphic organizers effectively. The teacher plays a crucial role in helping children learn the appropriate uses for graphic organizers. Teachers need to teach this skill specifically. Using graphic organizers appropriately can help children plan their work, monitor their progress, and summarize their information as a precursor for the Utilization and Application of Knowledge phase of learning (see Utilization and Application of Knowledge, page xxx).

Sharing Ideas and Findings

Children *share ideas and findings* with one another throughout the learning process. This is an important part of the collaborative work in any **Classroom Ready for In-depth Study.** James Britton (1970) reminds us of the importance of conversation in learning processes. In the inquiry process, children engage in open dialogue about their discoveries. As they share their ideas and findings, they develop their understanding of the topic in a way that will ultimately produce results and further hypotheses.

Key Points

- Inquiry-based classrooms provide multiple opportunities for children to discuss their learning activities with each other and with the teacher. Hall (1987) suggests that when children construct their own learning they are supporting the development of oral language skills. Teachers take on the role of facilitators of knowledge (Dewey, 1938/1997). Children most effectively construct knowledge in social contexts when they are working on something that is meaningful to them. In these situations, children talk about their work, clarify ideas, and make connections. Dialogue continues throughout the learning process. Inquiry-based classrooms provide avenues for children to summarize their learning by sharing their ideas and findings.
- Graphic organizers and non-linguistic representations increase children's recognition and retention of content (Marzano et al., 2001). Although these tools are useful during all parts of the instructional process to help children make connections to their prior learning as well as to summarize and elaborate on their learning (McTighe, 1992), graphic organizers and non-linguistic representations are particularly instrumental in helping children plan their work.

Suggestions

- K-W-H-L charts can help children articulate the planning process. They help children ask the following questions: "What do I **k**now? What do I **w**ant to know? **H**ow will I find what I want to learn? What did I **l**earn?" Children can use each of these steps to remain focused, using the answer to "What did I learn?" to apply to their final results.
- Practice asking open-ended questions. "What is your goal? What are you going to do with this information? How will you combine your ideas? Where will you look to find that information? What resource was the most helpful and why? What does this resource tell you? How are you thinking about designing your project? How could you summarize that? What questions do you have about this? Why? How?"
- Help children articulate their goals, their understandings, and their questions.
- Introduce graphic organizers to children gradually. Model the graphic organizers extensively. Teach children to use the graphic organizers to plan and/or to summarize their work. There are multiple resources for teachers to

use to access graphic organizers. Below is a partial list of sites that may be useful:

- www.enchantedlearning.com/graphicorganizers
- www.graphic.org
- http://edhelper.com/teachers/graphic_organizers.htm
- http://www.ncrel.org/sdrs/areas/issues/students/learning/lr1grorg.htm
- http://freeology.com/graphicorgs/

- Encourage children to work together to create a project, an artifact for display, or a summary of information. Incorporate tasks that will help the children organize their learning.
- Consider incorporating inquiry design into daily instruction through quick activities. For example, at the kindergarten level, have groups of three children organize various diverse materials into three different categories and explain their reasoning for the groups they created. The act of explanation solidifies the children's understanding of the "why" and the "how" behind their actions. Document this experience through photographs and captions representing children's explanations.
- Many times, children need encouragement to interact with one another. Children working in groups need time to establish relationships. Offer multiple opportunities for groups to work together so they learn to become productive. On the other hand, groups that are static for extended periods of time do not foster development of skills in flexibility and adaptability. Watch for indicators that it is time to change the group structure and provide new group membership opportunities.

Photos

Children are working together to sort a variety of geometric shapes into categories of their own design.

This child-generated graphic organizer compares two versions of *Charlie and the Chocolate Factory*, the movie and the book. The child's engagement is obvious.

Children work together to discover answers to their group question.

Children discuss their findings in an informal setting in the classroom.

Research Resources

In the child-centered classroom, the teacher is not the transmitter of knowledge; the child is the constructor of knowledge. The teacher stimulates interest in a particular concept, essential question, or core idea. Capitalizing on children's natural curiosity, the teacher provides a variety of sources of information about the topic. This information serves as a foundation for continuing cognitive development and it helps the child formulate new schema or elaborate on existing ones. The child does not sit back and absorb information; instead, the child constructs understanding by interacting with information (Piaget, 1955). In order to construct knowledge, however, a child must first have the physical resources to access information.

Multiple Computers Available

Computers allow children to interact with content. Desktop PCs and laptops are valuable tools for research. These can be arranged or available for work in workstations or centers to encourage collaboration and conversation as children explore concepts.

Multiple Research Books Available

Display a variety of non-fiction books for children to choose from when exploring topics of study. The pictures and text in these books provide multiple representations of the concepts and support children as they make connections to prior knowledge and develop new knowledge and understanding. Reference books such as dictionaries, encyclopedias, atlases, and topic-specific texts need to be accessible to the learner.

Multiple Resources on Topic of Study Available

It is vital that children have access to multiple sources of information in order to acquire knowledge on a subject and to develop the skills necessary to use that knowledge (See *Seeking Information,* page 161). Throughout the classroom, display a wide array of resources that relate to the topics of study. When possible, include authentic representations of topics associated with the study. Some children have limited experiences outside of their neighborhoods. Teachers can "bring the world into the classroom" in a variety of ways, but a child's direct experience with the specific topic or object of discussion is the best way to cultivate true understanding. Consider, for example, a reading lesson based on a book that compares cats' tails (animals) with cattails (plants). Some children involved in the lesson might not be able to comprehend the actual comparison because they are not familiar with cattails. Providing some actual cattails for the children to observe and discuss will support the children's understanding. It is worth the time it takes to collect authentic representations and objects that support the concepts a teacher wants to introduce to the children.

Resources should appeal to all modes of learning (Gardner, 1983). Include digital and print resources, books, data, photography, music, artwork, graphs, and charts. Children read and explore informational texts, investigate authentic artifacts, and participate in simulations. Guest speakers share information about the topic at hand. Make tools that support the exploration process (measurement tools, maps, and so on) available to the children. Inquiry-based learning uses all of these resources to answer the questions teachers and children pose about any given topic. Additionally, children can use these resources to explore the topic of study while engaging in active learning. They create products that result from their explorations.

Key Points

- Vary the resources the children use. It is important to include as many authentic resources as possible, especially for children in the primary grades whose ability to grasp abstract concepts is not as developed as that of older children (Piaget, 1955).
- Children need the skills to access information from multiple types of resources and time to explore the resources provided to them.

Suggestions

- People in the community can serve as pathways to enlarge the children's understanding. These "knowledgeable others" can provide valuable insight into many different topics of study.
- Teach children how to use resources. Each type of resource has its own features and presents information in a different way. Consider, for example, the contrast between a brochure and a textbook, a photograph and a chart, a letter that is an artifact and a summary of its contents (Mooney, 2001).
- Search the web for virtual tours of museums as well as photo exhibits and other similar programming. Children can explore these sites during a center activity.
- Provide the children with a narrow range of web resource options. Responses to a generic search are generally too broad for children to manage. Even older children spend far too much time in "hunting and gathering" mode to make this an effective use of their time. WebQuests are a focused tool that can teach children about accessing information. (See WebQuest.org for more details.) While such searches can be very useful for finding information, make sure that their specificity does not do away with the inquiry process.
- Simulations—creating a world within the classroom where children can role play, interact, and experience scenarios related to a certain topic of study—are a useful tool for inquiry-based processes. Although many are available for purchase, it is also possible to design simulations. Use, for example, Alice McLerran's book *Roxaboxen* as inspiration to design scenarios related to creating a town or community and the roles of community members. Many social studies concepts can be explored as children and teachers work together to recreate a community similar to the one found in the story.
- Field trips are a primary resource for children. If funding is an issue, consider designing virtual trips and using these "trips" as a focus for projects.
- Bring authentic artifacts to school for display and exploration.

Photos of Learners Involved in In-depth Study

Children use a whiteboard to explore
number sense together.

Experiments serve as authentic resources for discovery.

Hot Water

Cold Water

Science Journal
Ali   .ON

100 sheets • 200 pages
9½ x 7½ in/24.7 x 19.0 cm
wide ruled • 09910

Questions:
How do we know if it is cold?
How do we keep warm when it is cold?
How do we know if it is going to snow?

The teacher talks with children about a topic of exploration: snow. Children can extend their learning by having a first-hand experience with snow. Notice how one child documents the exploration process using a camera.

Computers can motivate children and offer an avenue for shared discovery of information.

Evidence of Inquiry-based Learning

Creating an intellectual environment that supports inquiry-based learning is essential for the teacher who wants to integrate the skills and objectives of various components of the curriculum. This is a major undertaking; for this reason, teachers must plan carefully. Teachers must consider the mandated curriculum as well as the developmental needs of the individual children when developing core learning goals and questions for the children to study. In this age of accountability, the expectation is that children will achieve the level of knowledge and understanding set forth through the curriculum. Additionally, teachers must strive to provide children with the experiences they need in order to develop the skills necessary to be active, independent learners.

It is possible to measure the progress toward these goals through the physical aspects of the classroom environment as well as through the children's work. In a classroom that engages children effectively in inquiry-based learning, children should be able to develop their understanding of specific topics of study, and then apply their knowledge of those topics. This does not mean that the children will just present information. Rather, it means that children will synthesize their understanding to create a product or something representative of their learning.

While there are many different models of inquiry-based learning, it is helpful to carefully define this type of learning process in terms of specific attributes that the teacher can observe and quantify. The *Primary Educators Environment Checklist* (see page 181), outlines four phases of inquiry based learning: *Seeking Information, In-depth Exploration, Asking Questions and Sharing Knowledge*, and *Utilization and Application of Knowledge*. There are descriptions of these phases and their associated indicators below. They are also summarized by Table III (see page 164).

Seeking Information

In many classrooms, *Seeking Information* may look similar to *Research Resources* (see page 153) in inquiry-based pedagogy. There is, however, a subtle and essential difference. The environmental aspect of *Research Resources* refers to physicality of the classroom and resources. *Seeking Information*, on the other hand, refers to children's ability to access the information available to them through those resources. While children are acquiring the information necessary to their exploration, they must use a variety of skills to make that information useful. The teacher's role is to introduce the children to the skills they need to organize information in a beneficial way. These skills are numerous. They include sequencing, skimming and scanning, comparing and contrasting, classifying, visualizing, analyzing, summarizing, and testing hypotheses (Marzano, Pickering, & Pollock, 2001). Children must understand and apply these skills as well as be able to integrate them into their learning experience in order to benefit from the exploration process.

In-depth Exploration

During the exploration phase, continue to frame the experience so that children are successful in constructing meaning. Children see success as they interact with the authentic materials provided to them. The children need time to explore these resources in a purposeful and focused way. Exploring these materials is the way children conduct research, sifting and sorting information to build cognitive connections. They benefit from having available to them a variety of tools. Set out magnifiers, measuring cups, rulers, and other similar materials in the classroom. Computers are another key resource children can use to expand their learning experiences.

To encourage children to participate in in-depth exploration, define the appropriate level of complexity for the task at hand. In a first-grade classroom, for example, teachers typically frame a science-based learning experience by asking the children about the attributes of plants. Then children explore these attributes by planting seeds. Through this activity, children observe the seeds growing and get first-hand knowledge of the parts of the plant and the conditions plants require to grow. While this is a good activity on its own, an interesting way to expand the children's exploration is to ask them to compare different plants as they grow from seeds, instead of just one plant variety. This experience is more complex. It requires greater use of research tools (magnifiers, measurement equipment, monitoring notebooks, graph paper, and so on) and requires children to synthesize more information. While both activities address the curricular objective, the second activity promotes deeper exploration of the topic and generates more connections to children's understanding of plants and the factors that affect plant growth.

Collaborative exploration is another component of this phase of inquiry. It is important to create learning groups that support the development of both academic and communication skills. Children should have many opportunities to talk about their observations. Dialogue that flows from child to child and from child to teacher serves as the cornerstone of the learning experience. Through this dialogue, children consolidate their observations into generalizations and design mental frameworks about the core concepts of the subject of inquiry.

Providing children with carefully selected topics and sufficient material for exploration helps those children become confident constructors of knowledge. In this way, children gain insight into different aspects of the topic. This also helps children connect the educational topic to their own experiences. This lays the foundation for *Asking Questions/Sharing Knowledge.*

Asking Questions/Sharing Knowledge

One goal of inquiry-based instruction is helping children formulate their own questions. This is a characteristic of an independent, productive thinker. Classroom frameworks that support collaborative learning result in active, rather than passive, learning. This process of collaborative problem-solving supports cognitive development, since it is rooted in articulation of ideas and concepts. Dialogue between the teacher and child, as well as between children themselves, will help solidify knowledge. By learning how to summarize the answers to their questions, children learn how to clarify their understanding. Children can create and share these summaries orally, in writing, or in pictorial or three-dimensional form.

Utilization and Application of Knowledge

While one outcome of inquiry-based instruction is the development of independent learners, it is important to acknowledge that an enormous number of skill sets must be in place to achieve that outcome.

The final aspect of Evidence of Inquiry-based Learning is *Utilization and Application of Knowledge.* During this phase, children begin to apply or use their understanding in new and useful ways.

Marzano and Kendall (2007) outline three categories of skills necessary for children to be able to apply their knowledge:

- Information, facts, and knowledge (What do I know?);
- Mental procedures for manipulation of that information (What do I do with it?); and
- Physical procedures for manipulation of the information (How do I do it?).

It is the teacher's responsibility to be sure that children have the information and resources they need in order to learn, as well as the skills they will require to work with the information they collect. Consider the example of first grade plant exploration, described above: in order for the children to learn from and use their experiences, they must have the skills of observation, measurement, documentation, and representation. The teacher must teach and model those skills.

The outcomes of the children's inquiries must be complex enough for the children to learn from, and yet the inquiries must remain developmentally appropriate. It is crucial not to confuse presentation of knowledge with real understanding. When teachers ask children to create a report about a topic, it simply encourages children to copy the information they find. For children to create a more complex product, such as a brochure, requires that they integrate both knowledge and process. In a true inquiry-based classroom, children create work on projects, debate ideas, solve problems, share hypotheses, create strategies, and develop skills (Bond, 2002) based on the information they gather and their understanding of the information. In an inquiry-based classroom, children's final products reflect a synthesis of content and process knowledge.

Table III (on the following page) summarizes the interactions between the teacher, the children, and the environment during the phases of the Inquiry Process identified through the *Primary Educator's Environment Checklist*.

Table III | Roles of Teachers, Children, and Environment During the Phases of the Inquiry Process

Phases of Inquiry Process	Indicators: Teacher	Indicators: Children	Indicators: Environment
Seeking Information	**The teacher is:** • Stimulating curiosity by framing relevant and interesting questions; • Scaffolding children's learning by helping them access prior knowledge, creating skill sets, and providing resources; and • Introducing ideas through dialogue, authentic materials, and sensory experiences.	**The children are:** • Exploring resources which stimulate the different modalities; • Working with computers; • Interacting with guest speakers; • Exploring authentic artifacts; taking field trips (virtual or authentic); and • Interacting with a variety of resources.	**The classroom has:** • Multiple resources including print materials, pictures, books, data, computers, audio and visual materials; and • Peripherals are connected to the area of study and primary resources are available.
In-depth Exploration	**The teacher is:** • Asking reflective, open-ended questions; • Grouping children in ways which support academic and communication development; and • Designing investigations that enrich vocabulary and help children construct meaning.	**The children are:** • Working with manipulatives; • Using tools to answer their questions; • Engaging in dialogue with one another and the teacher; and • Asking questions and creating hypotheses.	**The classroom has:** • Centers for exploration; • Purposeful dialogue; • Purposeful movement, associated with active learning; and • Tools for exploration (magnifiers, computers, measurement tools).
Formulating Questions and Sharing Knowledge	**The teacher is:** • Grouping the children for positive interactions; • Guiding the children by focusing their learning on specific objectives; and • Encouraging dialogue (child-to-child; child-to-teacher) through questioning.	**The children are:** • Asking questions; • Creating graphic organizers, classifying, predicting, and analyzing resources; and • Comparing their ideas with one another and with their own personal schema.	**The classroom has:** • Graphic organizers; • Summarizing tools; • Data collection books; • Tape recorders, a variety of cameras, video recorders; and • Presentation arena with documentation of learning.
Utilization and Application of Knowledge	**The teacher is:** • Structuring avenues for integration of knowledge; • Providing focus for learning; and • Helping children make connections to skill sets, prior knowledge, and content-area knowledge.	**The children are:** • Solving problems and representing solutions; • Synthesizing knowledge to create representations or products; • Demonstrating ownership of the learning; and • Using knowledge in ways which benefit others.	**The classroom has:** • Authentic products, products the children produced; • Incorporation of presentations; and • Application of knowledge in the school, home, and community.

Key Points

When analyzing classrooms using the *Primary Educator's Environment Checklist* (see page 181), one is able to place them on a continuum from teacher-centered (traditional) to child-centered (non-traditional or constructivist) based on the characteristics associated with the **Inquiry-based Learning Environment.** There are two underlying principles associated with this to keep in mind:

- The phases of this process are fluid. Children move between the different aspects of the inquiry-based model in an integrated rather than a linear way. Teachers must be adept at managing all levels of the process simultaneously because their children will be moving through them at different rates.
- An inquiry-based learning environment utilizes an integrated approach to teaching and learning that focuses on exploration and useful applications of discovery. It is an expression of "being" as much as it is a way of "doing."

Suggestions

- Move slowly. Think about teaching and learning. Use the *Primary Educator's Environment Checklist* to see if the classroom environment is supportive.
- Analyze a typical week in the classroom. Pay special attention to the following:
  - How much time do children spend talking about their work? How does this compare with the amount of time the teacher spends talking?
  - How do the children use graphic organizers and non-linguistic representations of concepts in the classroom? Do the children use a variety of graphic organizers independently and in collaborative groups for planning and for summarizing information?
  - How many resources are available for any topic of study? What types of resources are available? Are there multiple representations of the topic to help children make connections and solidify their understanding?
  - Do children have access to computers and web-based resources?
  - Are the children working in pairs and small groups?
  - Do children have the skills to frame their own questions for inquiry? Do they have the mental and procedural skill sets to synthesize, organize, apply, and present information? Are children using their knowledge in isolation, or are they using it in contextual ways?
  - Are authentic materials used as peripherals in the classroom? Do children create artifacts that portray the concepts of the study?

- Are children constructing meaning (vocabulary and information) through their interaction with the content and with one another?
- Integrating the arts into the learning process helps support inquiry-based learning. Through the arts, children can synthesize their knowledge and represent it in ways that appeal to their multiple intelligences (Gardner, 1983).
- Original skits, dioramas, web pages, advertisements, surveys, PowerPoint presentations, multimedia projects, and visuals, all are appropriate for presentations.
- Create surveys and tabulate results. Make summarizing statements about the results. Display these results as authentic information resources.
- Conduct experiments. The educational benefits of doing experiments with the children makes it well worth the time it takes to set them up.

Photos

Taking quick trips outside and writing down observations is one way to incorporate elements of inquiry-based learning.

Having children illustrate math concepts helps create engagement. This teacher incorporates authentic uses of math into her daily instruction.

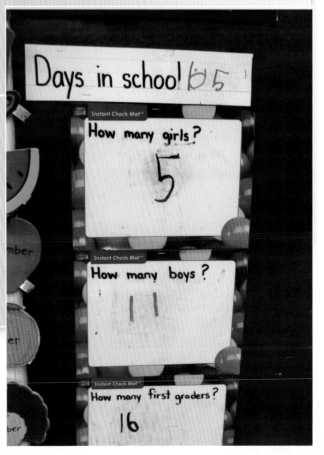

Notice the magnifiers. More than one child can explore the terrarium at a time for social learning. A book serves as an added resource.

Older children continue to explore the concepts of balance, measurement, and geometry by working with blocks and manipulatives.

Commentary

Teacher Comments

- Initially, I was overwhelmed by trying to incorporate the principles of inquiry-based learning throughout the day in my second-grade class. I tried to do too much all at once. I learned that you can't just start being an inquiry-based classroom. It's a process of becoming. I've moved along the continuum, but it has not been a linear process.
- I'm a very organized person and I liked the easy-to-follow design of traditional teaching; but, now that I have discovered the genuine learning that occurs through inquiry, I've abandoned the traditional design. I find I enjoy teaching more now. I think it's because my children enjoy learning more!
- When I realized that the children needed to learn skills for unlocking information, I was motivated to teach those specific skills in a variety of contexts. One thing that really made a difference was teaching them about the text forms and features associated with a variety of different genres. One example is skimming and scanning. Once my children became proficient with headings, captions, bulleted points, and so on, they became much more efficient at using written information.

Consultant Comment

- It is worth the time and effort to prepare the foundation, the classroom environment, to engage children in the process of learning. As early childhood educators, we focus on cooperation, not competition. When classrooms are designed according to early childhood learning principles, focusing on an inquiry-based process, children are able to learn at their individual levels. This allows them to challenge themselves to continue to grow and learn. A love of learning is clearly evident.

Principal Comments

- Teachers in our school had used graphic organizers for years. However, we found that their benefit was limited until the children started using them. All children learned to use designated graphic organizers in appropriate contexts. For example, children discovered that a Venn diagram worked better to compare information while a Fishbone organizer was more beneficial for showing cause and effect. Graphic organizers became a real support for learning when the children started to use them for planning their work and for organizing information.

- I wanted all our classrooms to reflect inquiry-based learning. I thought a couple of professional development sessions would take care of it. Boy, did I miss the boat. I now understand how the different aspects of the environment work together to support inquiry-based learning. I see teachers in my school are working toward inquiry-based learning. We use children's work as the evidence of our progress.

A Room to Learn

The Leader and Professional Development

Strategies for Change

Classroom environment has for years been a focus for early childhood programs. The schools of Reggio Emilia, Italy, for example, provide one of the more successful approaches to using the environment to support child development and learning. The preschools of Reggio Emilia highlight the importance of the classroom environment as a factor in teaching and learning in their statement that the environment functions as "the third teacher" (Gandini, 1998). This is a belief statement about the importance of the learning environment in early childhood classrooms that typically have one to two teachers. The environment functions as a partner, working with the early childhood teachers. Consider, then, how important it is as a tool for teaching and learning in a primary classroom that has only one teacher!

The environment is the foundation for child-centered instruction. This chapter provides tips and tools for creating an environment that reflects a constructivist philosophy. While there is no single pathway for moving from a traditional toward a constructivist classroom, using professional development and implementing useful environmental tools and strategies can help any teacher or program through the stages of this process. Below are some examples of processes that can help schools progress toward inquiry-based instruction.

The Leader's Role

The leader sets the tone and creates the climate in a school. The leader is the facilitator of facilitators. The leader is the one who knows the status of the organization, the achievement, needs, and interests of the children, and faculty strengths, interests, and needs. It is also important to know and understand the families and surrounding community in order to involve them in the educational process.

One of the main goals of any educational leader is to engage **all** children in meaningful learning. As the leader of an educational program, it is important to strive to do the following:

- Create a caring climate,
- Involve all stakeholders,
- Ask questions,
- Challenge thinking,
- Provide opportunities for professional development,
- Provide resources, and
- Plan for reflection and celebration.

Creating a caring climate begins with the leader. Modeling caring acts throughout the building and day sends the message that caring for one another is important. When leaders model caring for others, teachers and children follow suit. What better way to teach than by example? Principals can show children they care by welcoming them to school each morning as they arrive, visiting classrooms throughout the day, assisting in the lunchroom, inviting children to talk, being available for children to share successes with, and informally sharing children's successes with their families. An effective principal creates a climate where children, teachers, and families are excited about teaching and learning with one another.

Involve all stakeholders to create a sense of community. Create welcoming schools by involving faculty and staff, children, families, and community members in the learning process. Empower everyone to become a part of the learning community. Use shared leadership to create a vision and mission for the school that will guide and inspire **all** the stakeholders. Positive interactions and relationships and a shared vision are the building blocks of a caring learning community.

Ask questions, even if they are tough questions, to inspire thinking and collaboration. Questioning why we do things or the way we do things challenges people to think about potentially better ways. In safe learning communities questions are expected and valued as critical components in teaching and learning.

Challenge the thinking of children and teachers in the learning community. Asking children to talk about their learning experiences and their understanding of an activity or lesson helps the children process their learning and helps them develop communication skills. *Challenging the thinking* of teachers, in a safe and non-threatening way, encourages them to continuously reflect, discuss, problem-solve, and plan for quality learning experiences for **all** children.

Provide opportunities for professional development for teachers, independently and with others. Consider using faculty meetings for professional development in addition to sharing news and announcements. Use email for managerial news and information and faculty meetings for collaborating, learning new skills, discussions, debates, and reflecting upon teaching and learning experiences. Visiting one another's classrooms (as described below in the walkthrough process on page 176) provides valuable professional development without leaving the building. Consider partnering with other schools to provide opportunities for walkthroughs and in-depth explorations and collaboration.

Provide resources for change. Use the action plan forms provided in this book (*The Classroom Ready for Meaningful Learning; The Classroom Ready for Social Learning; The Classroom Ready for Purposeful Learning; The Classroom Ready for Responsible Learning; The Classroom Ready for Continuous Learning*; and *The Classroom Ready for Inquiry-based Learning*) to assist in planning for growth according to the *Primary Educator's Environment Checklist* (see page 181). Key steps in facilitating change include: developing action plans, identifying necessary resources, and locating or purchasing resources for teachers to implement their plans. Some school systems have skillful carpenters on the staff who can construct structures that will enhance the learning environment at low cost. When budgets are tight, families and community members serve as valuable resources.

Plan for reflection and celebration. Too often these two critical components get left out due to lack of time. Reflection serves as a guide. It is a useful process to think, re-think, and analyze. Educators can do this alone, in pairs, and in small or large groups. This should take place regularly. Find time or make time to reflect. Celebrate the learning. Share successes during faculty meetings. Post documentation in common areas and in the halls, sharing celebrations of learning so stakeholders can see, share, and learn from the successful learning experiences of others in the school. Celebrate learning with families and communities as well. Invite others to see the faculty and children engaged in dynamic learning experiences in the school.

Walkthrough Processes for Teacher Development

Schools require continuous development. Although the focus of each day's work is on the children, there is also a need to create a positive learning environment for adults. The teachers in the building need structures that support continuous learning. Workshops, book studies, continuing education, and coaching experiences all offer opportunities for teachers to increase their knowledge and skill base. However, considering the nature of teaching and learning and applying it to the adult learner, it becomes evident that informal frameworks are also helpful. Opportunities to work together, to reflect, to dialogue, and to observe are ways to support individual and total school growth (Lambert, 2003). The walkthrough is an experience that incorporates these informal frameworks for learning.

A number of authors (Downey, Steffy, English, Frase, and Poston, 2004; Love, 2009) have explored the various purposes and roles that walkthroughs play in school development. Walkthroughs are a useful way to gather data, to evaluate, to identify teaching points, and to observe child development. Recently, the walkthrough has become a tool administrators use to assess teachers. This is unfortunate because that process undermines the use of walkthroughs for developing a cohesive community of learners. The walkthrough process that supports the development of positive learning environments is not evaluative. Instead, it is a collaborative, regularly occurring experience for teachers.

When a walkthrough is a collaboration, it becomes an effective tool for individual growth and total school improvement (Lambert, 2003; Dufour and Eaker, 1998). Walkthroughs create an open environment in which teachers can share ideas and work together to create solutions to common problems. Walkthroughs can serve to reinforce concepts introduced in faculty meetings or in training sessions. In this way, walkthroughs give focus and direction, and lead to concrete changes in the classroom that demonstrate understanding of the abstract concepts presented during the workshop setting. The walkthrough is an extension of learning. It serves a strategic role by offering all educators a consistent level of understanding and familiarity with new educational concepts.

Teacher walkthroughs are like field trips. Through this experiential learning, teachers explore the organizational design and pedagogical practices that are the targeted areas for school improvement. When teams of teachers dialogue and reflect on their experience together, they articulate the essence of the school processes and increase their understanding about teaching and learning.

It is important to design a walkthrough so it is tailored to the learning climate and culture of the school as well as the learning styles and needs of the individual faculty members. Creating norms for conducting walkthroughs is important, especially in schools that do not enjoy collaborative learning environments. Suddenly implementing this process without preparing the faculty can create a culture of mistrust and divisiveness. It is vital to plan the walkthrough process with the faculty, and to take the time to establish the walkthrough's value to the teachers. Identify the specific areas of focus only after the faculty understands the procedures and purposes of the walkthrough.

The principal or director plays a key role in establishing the effective design and implementation of the walkthrough process (Ginsberg and Murphy, 2002). As the instructional leader, the principal makes many observations about the teaching and learning processes in the school. Observational tools are helpful for assessing school organizational design and instructional effectiveness. Use the *Primary Educator's Environment Checklist* (see page 181) to indentify (1) specific attributes of the classroom environment, and (2) processes for learning. With the use of this checklist, the principal or leadership team can systematically identify focus points for faculty development.

Walkthroughs that target specific attributes of the environment are a particularly effective use of the walkthrough process. First, the focus begins on the physical components of a classroom. Teachers perceive these components to be separate from their pedagogy, and therefore they are a less threatening area to address. One of the purposes of the environmental walkthrough is to quantify the value and benefit of the physical components of the classroom. Initially, the guiding principle of the walkthrough is: *If I don't see it, it's not there.* Applying this principle consistently helps teachers keep a pinpoint perspective on the physical aspect of the environment. Later, walkthroughs can focus on pedagogy in relation to the environment as a teaching tool.

Administrators can use any number of different checklists and even computer programs to guide walkthroughs. The danger is that these processes often produce large quantities of data without effectively improving teachers' skills and attitudes. Walkthroughs are effective tools for change when teachers work together to answer a reflective question that focuses on an area of growth for the school. Use the *Primary Educator's Environment Checklist* to generate precise and useful questions (see samples below). These questions guide the walkthrough process and help teachers develop a deeper understanding of how their classroom environments function. This understanding promotes positive changes in instructional practices.

The instructional leader selects teams of teachers to address each topic question. Teams of no more than four teachers should observe classrooms throughout the school. This small group reduces the amount of distraction to the teaching-learning process and encourages productive dialogue following the observation. It is a good idea to share the focus question in advance with the group of observers as well as with those whose classrooms are being observed. This is not intended to be a "gotcha" process. Conduct walkthroughs weekly to provide all teachers the opportunity to take several learning trips through the school. It is not necessary for all teachers to participate in a walkthrough for each topic of focus, although there are some topics which may need that level of reinforcement.

Prior to beginning the walkthrough, teachers meet with the principal, or the designated instructional leader, to discuss the guiding question for the experience. During this discussion process, it may come out that some of the teachers define terms differently. Having this pre-walkthrough session helps teachers develop common definitions of terms. For example, the question "What structures are in place to help children articulate their learning?" (see *Sample Questions Regarding the Physical Environment),* can cause a great deal of discussion. Teachers may spend time debating what constitutes evidence of "articulation of learning." These conversations serve to solidify teachers' understandings about the concept and to reinforce the value of incorporating it into their teaching.

During the walkthrough, teachers focus on the selected question by writing down their thoughts and observations in anecdotal, descriptive form. At the conclusion of the classroom visits, teachers come together to reflect upon the data that was gathered during the walkthrough. The teachers discuss and chart their findings. For example, if the focus question is: "What evidence is there of children engaging in social learning?" the teachers may provide observations such as: "The children worked in groups. The arrangement of chairs in small groupings promoted social learning experiences. The children were discussing topics of study. The children were exploring and researching topics in teams. Groups of children were creating peripherals."

At the conclusion of the walkthrough experience, teachers write their personal reflections and identify their own next steps. Guide the teachers' reflections by asking the following: "What change will you make in the way you are teaching or structuring your classroom as a result of this walkthrough?" The principal or instructional leader of the walkthrough uses this information to support teachers in their personal growth process and to plan future professional development.

Several sample reflective questions for walkthroughs based on the *Primary Educator's Environment Checklist* are below. Notice that some of these questions are observational questions that allow for data collection. Others require "wrestling" with underlying pedagogical concepts. As teachers become more adept at observation, reflection, and dialogue about what they see, it will become easier to introduce higher-order questions into the walkthrough process.

Sample Questions Regarding the Physical Environment

1. What components of a healthy environment are present? What components are lacking? Focus on well-maintained furniture, smell, temperature, cleanliness, safety, and nourishment.

2. What types of lighting do we have in our classrooms? What is the ratio of natural lighting to other types of lighting? What evidence is there that supplemental lighting is purposeful?

3. What are the indicators that our environments are welcoming and inviting? What structures do we use to create a sense of community?

4. How does the design of the classroom support social learning? What types of learning spaces are included in our classrooms (individual spaces, small group space, large group space, meeting spaces)?

5. What centers are available for exploratory learning?

6. What do the peripherals say about teaching and learning?

7. What structures help to organize the materials and resources in the classroom?

Sample Questions Regarding the Learning in the Classroom

1. What structures are in place to help children articulate their learning?

2. What authentic artifacts are available for child exploration?

3. What evidence indicates that this is a child-centered environment?

4. How are our children accessing information? What resources are the children using?

5. What evidence indicates that in-depth exploration is taking place in the classroom?

6. In what ways are the children applying the knowledge they gain?

7. What evidence indicates that the children are engaging in meaningful learning?

Primary Educator's Environment Checklist

Use the following checklist as a tool to assess the following components of the primary classroom environment: Meaningful Learning, Social Learning, Purposeful Learning, Responsible Learning, Continuous Learning, and Inquiry-based Learning. Each type of learning has associated indicators. In order to administer the checklist, examine the classroom from a variety of focal points around the room, as well as from the heights of a child and adult. Sit in children's chairs and on the floor to simulate a child's perspective of the classroom. Assess indicators of each specific component (meaningful learning, social learning, purposeful learning, responsible learning, continuous learning, and inquiry-based learning) and rate each indicator with the appropriate score: 2, 1, or 0. A score of 2 indicates that an indicator is easily observed with strong physical evidence; a score of 1 indicates that an indicator is somewhat observable; and a score of 0 indicates that there is no physical evidence of the indicator. Each page of the *Primary Educator's Environment Checklist* contains space for notes. Use this area to document examples of evidence that support the indicators. After assessing all the components, calculate the score for each component or type of learning. Record the scores on the final page of the checklist. Consider having three people, a teacher, an administrator, and a consultant, fill out the checklist separately, and then come together to compare and discuss the results. This is a great way to develop plans of action for initiating change. Use the *Primary Educator's Environment Checklist* to facilitate teacher development and assist in creating classrooms that use the environment as a teaching tool.

Primary Educator's Environment Checklist

Rating Scale:

2=Evidence easily observable

1= Evidence somewhat observable

0=Evidence not observable

Meaningful Learning Environment

Foundational Elements for Physically and Emotionally Safe Classrooms

	The Healthy Classroom		The Welcoming Classroom
	Well-Maintained		**Color**
	Safe		Neutral Paint Color
	Well-Maintained Furniture		**Welcoming and Inviting**
	Well-Ventilated		Music
	Healthy Temperature (70°F)		Living Plants
	Pleasant–Smelling		Home-like Elements (pictures, softness)
	Lighting		**Sense of Community**
	Natural Light		Photos of Learners
	Varied Lighting		Procedures Created Together and Posted
	Nourishment		Planning Boards/Agendas
	Water Available		Artifacts Representing Learning Together
	Healthy Snacks		

Notes:

Primary Educator's Environment Checklist

Rating Scale:

2=Evidence easily observable

1= Evidence somewhat observable

0=Evidence not observable

Social Learning Environment			
The Classroom Arranged for Learning and Positive Learning Interactions			
	Room Arrangement		Seating Choices
	Individual Spaces		Table Space
	Small Group Spaces		Floor Space
	Large Group Work Space		Dyad and Triad Space
	Large Group Meeting Space		Variety of Seating Choices
	Child Work Space is the Focus of the Room Arrangement		Flexible Placements for Seating

Notes:

Primary Educator's Environment Checklist

Rating Scale:

2=Evidence easily observable

1= Evidence somewhat observable

0=Evidence not observable

Purposeful Learning Environment			
The Organized Classroom Physically Arranged for Focused Learning			
Learning Centers and Stations		**Teacher Space**	
	Clearly Defined Areas for Learning		Organized
	Literacy Centers		Flexible Space
	Shelving Divides Space and Allows for Visibility		Occupies Limited Amount of Physical Space
	Content Exploratory Areas Visible		
	Centers Arranged Loud/Quiet		
Personal Space for Children			
	Storage for Personal Belongings		
	Storage for Child Work (Portfolios, Learning Artifacts)		
	Display Space for Projects in Process and Finished Work		

Notes:

Primary Educator's Environment Checklist

Rating Scale:

2=Evidence easily observable

1= Evidence somewhat observable

0=Evidence not observable

Responsible Learning Environment			
Organized Materials in the Classroom to Promote Engagement in Learning			
Clutter		**Organized Materials**	
	Uncluttered and Clean		Clearly Arranged for Quick Access
	Materials Appropriate for Learning Centers/Stations		Easily Identifiable by Children
	Materials Focused on Current Learning Objectives		Organized in Containers for Easy Transport
Materials Available for Learning			Materials Safely Arranged
	Limited Number of Commericially Purchased Materials		Visibility of Materials Is Not Over-stimulating
	Limited Number of Worksheets Utilized for Learning		
	Textbooks Utilized as Resources, Not Main Tool for Driving Instruction		

Notes:

Primary Educator's Environment Checklist

Rating Scale:

2=Evidence easily observable

1= Evidence somewhat observable

0=Evidence not observable

Continuous Learning Environment			
Classroom Peripherals Representing the Learning Process and Learning Projects			
Commercial Peripherals		**Peripherals Representative of Learning**	
	Limited Commercial Materials on the Walls		Skills for Living and Learning Represented
	Nothing Hanging from the Ceiling		Authentic Work Displayed
Documentation of Learning			Learning Documentation Displayed for Use as a Resource or Learning Tool
	Variety of Assessments Utilized to Drive Instruction		
	Artifacts Represent Current Study		
	Photos of Learning in Process		

Notes:

Primary Educator's Environment Checklist

Rating Scale:

2=Evidence easily observable

1= Evidence somewhat observable

0=Evidence not observable

Inquiry-based Learning Environment				
The Classroom Ready for In-depth Study				
	Planning and Collaboration		**Evidence of Inquiry-based Learning**	
	Evidence of Conversations		Seeking Information	
	Evidence of Planning		In-depth Exploration	
	Evidence of Graphic Organizer Use		Asking Questions/Sharing Knowledge	
	Evidence of Sharing of Ideas and Findings		Utilization and Application of Knowledge	
	Research Resources			
	Multiple Computers Available			
	Multiple Research Books Available			
	Multiple Resources Available on Topic of Study			

Notes:

TOTALS		
Meaningful Learning Score –	_____	/Out of a possible 34
Social Learning Score –	_____	/Out of a possible 20
Purposeful Learning Score –	_____	/Out of a possible 22
Responsible Learning Score –	_____	/Out of a possible 22
Continuous Learning Score –	_____	/Out of a possible 16
Inquiry-based Learning Score –	_____	/Out of a possible 22

The higher the score in each area, the more child-centered the educational experience taking place there, and the more effectively educators and children are using the environment as a teaching tool.

Action Plans

On the following pages you will find forms that provide ways to reflect on and explore the results of the *Primary Educator's Environment Checklist*. Use these forms to create action plans for growth that address areas identified on the checklist with a score of 1 or 0, and to determine what resources a classroom needs to accomplish those plans. The forms cover the following topics:

- The Classroom Ready for Meaningful Learning
- The Classroom Ready for Social Learning
- The Classroom Ready for Purposeful Learning
- The Classroom Ready for Responsible Learning
- The Classroom Ready for Continuous Learning
- The Classroom Ready for Inquiry-based Learning

It is important to assess the classroom using the entire checklist. Once this has been done, select a component to focus on for growth. Focus on one Action Plan at a time, ending with the *Inquiry-based Learning Environment* component. Just as when working with children, each teacher should determine a process appropriate to her or his own learning style and personality, in collaboration with the principal or instructional leader.

The Classroom Ready for Meaningful Learning

Indicators	Action Plans
Healthy Classroom Well-maintained, safe, well-ventilated, healthy temperature, pleasant smelling, natural light, varied light, water and snacks available	
Welcoming Classroom Neutral paint color on the walls, music, living plants, home-like elements, photos of children, procedures created together, planning boards and agendas, artifacts representing learning together	

Materials Requested to Support the Action Plan	

The Classroom Ready for Social Learning

Indicators	Action Plans
Room Arrangement Individual spaces, small group work space, large group work space, large group meeting space (Student workspace is the focus of the room arrangement.)	
Seating Choices Table space, floor space, dyad/triad space, variety of seating options, flexible placements for seating	

Materials Requested to Support the Action Plan	

The Classroom Ready for Purposeful Learning

Indicators	Action Plans
Learning Centers and Stations Clearly defined areas for learning, literacy centers, shelving that divides space and allows for visibility, content exploratory areas visible, centers arranged for quiet and active work	
Personal Space for Students Storage for personal belongings, storage for student work (portfolios, learning artifacts), display space for projects in process and finished work	
Teacher Space Organized, flexible space, occupies limited amount of physical space	

Materials Requested to Support the Action Plan	

The Classroom Ready for Responsible Learning

Indicators	Action Plans
Clutter Uncluttered, clean, materials appropriate for learning centers/stations, materials focused on current learning activities and objectives	
Materials Available for Learning Limited number of commercially purchased materials, limited number of worksheets utilized for learning, textbooks function as resources rather than the main instructional tool	
Organized Materials Clearly arranged for quick access, easily identifiable by students, organized in containers for easy transport, materials safely arranged, visibility of materials is not over-stimulating	
Materials Requested to Support the Action Plan	

Indicators	Action Plans
Commercial Peripherals Limited commercial materials on the walls, nothing hanging from the ceiling	
Documentation of Learning Variety of assessment utilized to drive instruction, artifacts represent current study, photos of learning in process	
Peripherals Representative of Learning Documents demonstrating students' skills for life and learning on display throughout the room, authentic work on display, displayed learning documentation usable as a resource or learning tool	

Materials Requested to Support the Action Plan

The Classroom Ready for Inquiry-based Learning

Indicators	Action Plans
Planning and Collaboration Evidence of conversations, evidence of planning, evidence of graphic organizer use	
Research Resources Multiple computers available, multiple research books available, multiple resources available on topic of study	
Evidence of Inquiry-based Learning Seeking information, in-depth exploration, asking questions, utilization and application of knowledge	
Materials Requested to Support the Action Plan	

Leader's Quest and Future for Early Childhood Education in Primary Schools

More now than ever, primary classrooms need leaders who can support teachers' efforts to stimulate positive change by enhancing learning experiences and engaging **all** children in the classroom. Just as teachers excite children about the learning process and motivate those children to question, explore, reflect, and understand, educational leaders must serve in a similar role for teachers.

According to the National Association of Early Childhood Teacher Educators (NAECTE) *Position Statement on Early Childhood Certification for Teachers of Children 8 Years Old and Younger in Public School Settings* (2009), "NAECTE recommends that state certification agencies and school districts adopt the following policies:

- Require an early childhood certificate and/or endorsement for those teaching in classrooms for children 5 years old and younger in state-funded pre-kindergarten and in kindergarten programs.
- Give priority in hiring and placement to teachers with an early childhood certificate and/or endorsement for public school classrooms for 6-, 7-, and 8-year-olds (first, second, and third grades).
- Require that early childhood certification and/or endorsement be based on completion of teacher preparation programs that meet professional preparation standards consistent with those established by the National Association for the Education of Young Children (NAEYC)" (p. 188).

Most kindergarten through third-grade public school teachers meet the legal definition of "highly qualified," yet these same teachers may not have received their teacher endorsement in an early childhood teacher preparation program. NAECTE recognizes and addresses this in their 2009 position statement. It is critical that early childhood (pre-K through third grade) teachers are prepared with an excellent knowledge of and skills in child development, be familiar with the latest research on the brain, and understand how young children need to learn and grow in this 21st century. It is important that early childhood professionals follow NAECTE's recommendation by giving priority in hiring to those with an early childhood certificate in first through third grade classrooms, and requiring an early childhood certificate for those teaching in classrooms with children in kindergarten or younger classes.

It is important to recognize, however, that many highly skilled teachers who do not have early childhood training are currently working in pre-kindergarten through third-grade classrooms. In the end, the goal must be that children in pre-kindergarten through third-grade classrooms receive the best educational opportunities possible, in environments that encourage and support each individual child. It is our hope that all teachers will fully utilize the environment as a teaching tool!

A Room to Learn

References

Akpinar, B. (2005). The role of sense of smell on learning and the effects of aroma on in cognitive learning. Pakistan Journal of Social Science, 3(7) 952–960. Retrieved online from http://docsdrive.com/pdfs/medwelljournals/pjssci/2005/952–960.pdf.

Bernath, P., and W. Masi. 2006. Smart school snacks: A comprehensive preschool nutrition education program. *Young Children* 61(3): 20–24.

Biological Science Currculum Study (BSCS, the SCI Center). 2001. *Profiles in science: A guide to NSF–funded high school instructional materials.* Colorado Springs, CO: BSCS.

Birren, F. 1978. *Color and human response.* New York: Van Nostrand Reinhold.

Bond, T. 2002. Information usage: The two shoppers analogy. Quality Education Support and Training. www.ictnz.com/articles/2shoppers.htm

Bredekamp, S., and C. Copple, eds. 1997. *Developmentally appropriate practice in early childhood programs.* Washington, DC: National Association for the Education of Young Children.

Bredekamp, S., and T. Rosegrant. 1992. *Reaching potentials: Appropriate curriculum and assessment for young children.* Washington, DC: National Association for the Education of Young Children.

Britton, J. 1970. *Language and learning.* Coral Gables, FL: University of Miami Press.

Bronson, M. B. 2000. Recognizing and supporting the development of self–regulation in young children. *Young Children* 55(2): 32–37.

Brooks, J., and M. Brooks. 2001. *In search of understanding: The case for constructivist classrooms.* Upper Saddle River, NJ: Prentice Hall.

Bruner, J. 1966. *Toward a theory of instruction.* Cambridge, MA: Harvard University Press.

Bruner, J. 1983. *Child's talk: Learning to use language.* New York: Norton.

Copple, C., and S. Bredekamp, eds. 2009. *Developmentally appropriate practice in early childhood programs.* Washington, DC: National Association for the Education of Young Children.

Dangel, J. R., E. Guyton, and C. B. McIntyre. 2003. Constructivist pedagogy in primary classrooms: Learning from teachers and their classrooms. *Journal of Early Childhood Teacher Education* 24(4), 237–245.

DeVries, R., and C. Kamii. 1980. *Group games in early education: Implications of Piaget's theory.* Washington, DC: National Association for the Education of Young Children.

DeVries, R., B. Zan, C. Hildebrandt, R. Edmiaston, and C. Sales. 2002. *Developing constructivist early childhood curriculum: Practical principles and activities.* New York, NY: Teachers College Press.

Dewey, J. 1899. *The school and society.* Chicago, IL: University of Chicago Press.

Dewey, J. 1910. *How we think.* Boston, MA: D.C. Heath.

Dewey, J. 1916. *Democracy and education.* New York, NY: MacMillan.

Dewey, J. 1938/1997. *Experience and education.* New York, NY: Simon & Schuster.

Dhong, H. J., S. K. Chung, and R. L. Doty. 1999. Estrogen protects against 3–methylindole–induced olfactory loss. *Brain Research* 824(2): 312–315.

Diamond, M. C. 2006. What are the determinants of children's academic successes and difficulties? New Horizons for Learning. http://home.blarg.net/~building/neuro/ diamond_determinants.htm

Diamond, M. C., and J. Hopson. 1998. *Magic trees of the mind: How to nurture your child's intelligence, creativity, and healthy emotions from birth through adolescence.* New York, NY: Penguin Putnam.

Diamond, M. C., D. Krech, and M. R. Rosenzweig. 1964. The effects of an enriched environment on the histology of the rat cerebral cortex. *The Journal of Comparative Neurology* 123(1): 111–119.

Downey, C. J., B. E. Steffy, F. W. English, L. E. Frase, and W. K. Poston. 2004. *The three–minute classroom walk–through: Changing school supervisory practice one teacher at a time.* Thousand Oaks, CA: Corwin Press.

DuFour, R., and R. Eaker. 1998. *Professional learning communities at work: Best practices for enhancing student achievement.* Bloomington, IN: National Educational Service.

Dunn, R., K. Dunn, and J. Perrin. 1994. *Teaching young children through their individual learning styles.* Boston, MA: Allyn & Bacon.

Dunn, R., J. S. Krimsky, J. B. Murray, and P. J. Quinn. 1985. Light up their lives: A research on the effects of lighting on children's achievement and behavior. *The Reading Teacher* 38(19): 863–869.

Eisenberg, N., and P. H. Mussen. 1989. *The roots of prosocial behavior in children*. New York, NY: Cambridge University Press.

Evanshen, P. 2010. Quality learning environments in the primary school: Incorporating best practices to engage learners. In F. Andersen, L. Hvidtved, and G. Kragh–Müller, eds. *Good learning environments for children.* Copenhagen, Denmark: Reitzels Forlag.

Fogarty, R. 1999. Architects of the mind. *Educational Leadership* (57)3: 76–78.

Forman, G., and B. Fyfe. 1998. Negotiated learning through design, documentation, and discourse. In C. Edwards, L. Gandini, and G. Forman, eds. *The hundred languages of children: The Reggio Emilia approach—advanced reflections.* Greenwich, CT: Ablex.

Fosnot, C. T. 2005. *Constructivism: Theory, perspectives, and practice* (2nd ed). New York, NY: Teachers College Press.

Gandini, L. 1998. Educational and caring spaces. In C. Edwards, L. Gandini, and G. Forman, eds. *The hundred languages of children: The Reggio Emilia approach—advanced reflections.* Greenwich, CT: Ablex.

Gardner, H. 1983. *Frames of mind: The theory of multiple intelligences*. New York, NY: Basic Books.

Gardner, H. 1991. *The unschooled mind: How children think and how schools should teach*. New York, NY: Basic Books.

Ginsberg, M. B., and D. Murphy. 2002. How walkthroughs open doors. *Educational Leadership* 59(8): 34–36.

Greenman, J. 1988. *Caring spaces, learning places: Children's environments that work*. Redmond, WA: Exchange Press.

Hall, N. 1987. *The emergence of literacy*. Portsmouth, NH: Heinemann Educational Books.

Hannaford, C. 2005. *Smart moves: Why learning is not all in your head*. Salt Lake City, UT: Great River Books.

Hart, L. 1998. *Human brain and human learning*. Kent, WA: Books for Educators.

Hathaway, W. E. 1987. Effects of light and color on pupil achievement, behavior and physiology. *Educational Facility Planner*. 25(2): 34.

Hathaway, W. E., J. A. Hargreaves, G. W. Thompson, and D. Novitsky. 1992. *A study into the effects of light on children of elementary school age: A case of daylight robbery*. Edmonton, Alberta, Canada: Alberta Education.

Henson, K. T. 2003. Foundations for learner–centered education: A knowledge base. *Education* 124(1): 5–16.

Herz, R. S. 2009. Aromatherapy facts and fictions: A scientific analysis of olfactory effects on mood, physiology and behavior. *International Journal of Neuroscience* 119: 263–290.

Herzog, M., ed. 1997. *Inside learning network schools.* Katonah, NY: Richard C. Owen Publishers.

Heschong Mahone Group. 1999. Daylighting in schools: An investigation into the relationship between daylighting and human performance. Fair Oaks, CA: Pacific Gas and Electric Company. www.h–m–g.com/downloads/Daylighting/ order_daylighting.htm

Hileman, S. 2006. Motivating students using brain–based teaching strategies. *The Agricultural Education Magazine* 78: 18–20. January–February.

Hillman, C. B. 1989. Creating a learning climate for the early childhood years. *Fastback Series* 292. Bloomington, IN: Phi Delta Kappa Educational Foundation.

Honey, P., and A. Mumford. 1982. *The manual of learning styles*. Maidenhead, UK: Peter Honey Publications.

Hubert, D. 1995. The flat stanley project. www.flatstanley.com

Irlen, H. 1991. *Reading by the colors: Overcoming dyslexia and other reading disabilities through the Irlen method*. New York, NY: Avery Publishing Group.

Isbell, R., and B. Exelby. 2001. *Early learning environments that work*. Silver Spring, MD: Gryphon House, Inc.

Jensen, E. 1994. *The learning brain*. Del Mar, CA: Turning Point Publishing.

Jensen, E. 1998 (revised, 2005). *Teaching with the brain in mind*. Alexandria, VA: ASCD.

Jensen, E. 2000. *Brain–based learning*. San Diego, CA: The Brain Store.

Jensen, E. 2001. *Arts with the brain in mind*. Alexandria, VA: ASCD.

Jensen, E. 2003. *Environments for learning*. San Diego, CA: The Brain Store.

Jensen, E. 2008. *Brain–based learning: The new paradigm of teaching*. Thousand Oaks, CA: Corwin Press.

Jonassen, D. 1991. Objectivism vs. constructivism: Do we need a new philosophical paradigm? *Educational Technology Research and Development* 39(3): 5–13.

Karplus, R., and H. Thier. 1967. *A new look at elementary school science*. Chicago, IL: Rand–McNally & Company.

Katz, L. G. 1998. What can we learn from Reggio Emilia? In C. Edwards, L. Gandini, and G. Forman, eds. *The hundred languages of children: The Reggio Emilia approach—advanced reflections.* Greenwich, CT: Ablex.

Katz, L. G., and S. Chard. 1996. *The contribution of documentation to the quality of early childhood education*. ERIC Digest. Champaign, IL: ERIC Clearinghouse on Elementary and Early Childhood Education.

Kempermann, G., H. G. Kuhn, and F. H. Gage. 1997. More hippocampal neurons in adult mice living in an enriched environment. *Nature* 386: 493–495.

King–Sears, M. 2007. Designing and delivering learning center instruction. *Intervention in School and Clinic* 42(3): 137–147.

Kolb, D. A. 1984. *Experiential learning: Experience as the source of learning and development*. Upper Saddle River, NJ: Prentice Hall.

Kolb, D. A., and R. Fry. 1975. Toward an applied theory of experiential learning. In C. Cooper, ed. *Theories of group processes.* London, UK: John Wiley.

Kovalik, S. J. 1993. *ITI: The model: Integrated thematic instruction*. Village of Oak Creek, AZ: Susan Kovalik and Associates.

Kovalik, S. J., and K. D. Olsen. 2005. *Exceeding expectations: A user's guide to implementing brain research in the classroom.* Covington, WA: Susan Kovalik & Associates.

Lambert, L. 2003. *Leadership capacity for lasting school improvement.* Alexandria, VA: ASCD.

Levine, S., and C. Coe. 1989. Endocrine regulation. In S. Cheren, ed., *Psychosomatic Medicine.* Madison, CT: International Universities Press.

Love, N., ed. 2009. *Using data to improve learning: A collaborative inquiry approach.* Thousand Oaks, CA: Corwin Press.

Marzano, R. J. 2003. *What works in schools: Translating research into action*. Alexandria, VA: ASCD.

Marzano, R. J., and J. S. Kendall. 2007. *The new taxonomy of educational objectives* (2nd ed). Thousand Oaks, CA: Corwin Press.

Marzano, R. J., D. J. Pickering, and J. E. Pollock. 2001. *Classroom instruction that works: Research–based strategies for increasing student achievement.* Alexandria, VA: ASCD.

Maslow, A. H. 1943. A theory of human motivation. *Psychological Review* 50: 370–396.

Maslow, A. 1987. *Motivation and personality* (3rd ed). New York, NY: Harper & Row.

McLerran, A. 1991. *Roxaboxen*. New York, NY: HarperCollins.

McTighe, J. 1992. Graphic organizers: Collaborative links to better thinking. In T. Worsham, ed. *Enhancing thinking through cooperative learning*. New York, NY: Teachers College Press.

Montessori, M. 1949. *The absorbent mind*. London, UK: Clio Press.

Mooney, M. E. 2001. *Text forms and features.* Katonah, NY: Richard C. Owen Publishers.

Morrison, G. 2000. *Teaching in America*. Boston, MA: Allyn and Bacon.

National Association of Early Childhood Teacher Educators (NAECTE) Position Statement in Public School Settings. 2009. *Journal of Early Childhood Teacher Education* 30(2): 186–187.

National Association for the Education of Young Children. 2003. Early childhood curriculum, assessment, and program evaluation: Building an effective, accountable system in programs for children birth through age 8. www.naeyc.org/files/naeyc/file/positions/CAPEexpand. pdf

Nelsen, J., L. Lott, and S. Glenn. 2000. *Positive discipline in the classroom.* Roseville, CA: Prima Publishing.

Newmann, F. M., B. A. Smith, E. Allensworth, and A. S. Bryk. 2001. *School instructional program coherence: Benefits and challenges.* Chicago, IL: Consortium on Chicago School Research. January 2001.

Nord, M., M. Andrews, and S. Carlson. 2009. *Household food security in the United States, 2008.* ERR–83, U.S. Dept. of Agriculture, Econ. Res. Serv. November 2009.

Olds, A. R. 2001. *Child care design guide.* New York, NY: McGraw–Hill.

Pauli, P., L. E. Bourne Jr., H. Diekmann, and N. Birbaumer. 1999. Cross–modality priming between odors and odor–congruent words. *American Journal of Psychology* 112(2): 175–186.

Piaget, J. 1955. *The construction of reality in the child.* London, UK: Routledge and Kegan Paul

Piaget, J. 1963. *The origins of intelligence in children*. New York, NY: W. W. Norton & Company, Inc.

Project Zero and Reggio Children, Italy. 2001. *Making learning visible: Children as individual and group learners.* Reggio Emilia, Italy: Reggio Children S.r.l. and Reggio Children/USA.

Rushton, S., and E. Larkin. 2001. Shaping the learning environment: Connecting developmentally appropriate practices to brain research. *Early Childhood Education Journal* 29(1): 25–33.

Rushton, S., J. Eitelgeorge, and R. Zickafoose. 2003. Connecting Brian Cambourne's conditions of learning theory to brain/mind principles: Implications for early childhood educators. *Early Childhood Education Journal* 31(1): 11–21.

Singer, D., and T. Revenson. 1996 (revised ed). *A Piaget primer: How a child thinks*. New York, NY: Plume.

Sousa, D. 2001. *How the brain learns.* Thousand Oaks, CA: Corwin Press.

Sylwester, R. 1995. *A celebration of neurons.* Alexandria, VA: ASCD.

Tarr, P. 2004. Consider the walls. *Young Children* 59(3): 88–92.

Taylor, A., and G. Gousie. 1988. The ecology of learning environments for children. *Educational Facility Planner* 26(4): 23–28.

Trawick–Smith, J. 1992. How the classroom environment affects play and development: Review of research. *Dimensions* 20(2): 27–30.

Vygotsky, L. 1962. *Thought and language.* Cambridge, MA: MIT Press.

Vygotsky, L. S. 1978. *Mind and society: The development of higher mental processes*. Cambridge, MA: Harvard University Press.

Weiler, K. 2004. What can we learn from progressive education? *Radical Teacher,* March 22.

Welch, W. W., L. E. Klopfer, G. S. Aikenhead, and J. T. Robinson. 1981. The role of inquiry in science education: Analysis and recommendations. *Science Education* 65(1): 33–50.

Wilkins, A. J., I. M. Nimmo–Smith, A. I. Slater, and L. Bedocs. 1989. Fluorescent lighting, headaches and eye strain. *Lighting Research and Technology* 21: 11–18.

Wolfe, P. 2001. *Brain matters: Translating research into classroom practice.* Alexandria, VA: ASCD.

Wolverton, B. C., Johnson, A., & Bounds, K. (1989). Interior landscape plants for indoor air pollution abatement. NASA/ALCA Final Report, *Plants for Clean Air Council,* Davidsonville, Maryland: U.S.

Index